Academic Life Coach 1.0 Training Guide

4th Edition

John Andrew Williams

Co-Founder, Coach Training EDU

Academic Life Coach 1.0 Training Guide

Academic Life Coach 1.0 Training Guide. Fourth Edition.
Copyright 2018 by John Andrew Williams.

To contact John Andrew Williams about Academic Life Coach training or upcoming events, please visit www.johnandrewwilliams.com.

A Publication of
Academic Life Coaching Inc.
1 Montello Avenue
Hood River, Oregon, 97031

4th Edition
September 15, 2018

also by John Andrew Williams:

Future-Proofed

The Academic Life Coaching Student Workbook

Essential Life Coaching

Core Motivation

For my two girls,
Paloma and Georgiana

TABLE OF CONTENTS

Preface

I consider my teaching career a happy accident. While I was still an undergraduate student, a friend and mentor decided last minute that he didn't have time to teach Latin at a local high school. He recommended me, and I got the gig.

For an undergraduate college student, the job paid well, and getting paid to teach a subject I loved seemed too good to be true. I immediately fell in love with teaching, and I enjoyed working with high school students. One year of teaching led to another. I taught Latin for six years, two in Rhode Island and four in southern Oregon.

If you ever have the opportunity to visit the Rogue Valley in southern Oregon, the geography is very much like Tolkien's Shire, with mountains on either side sheltering a beautiful, idyllic valley. It was in such an environment that I stumbled upon life coaching and the notion to combine it with the work I was doing with students. I was a mad-scientist in my teaching, trying out coaching concepts and ideas with students, designing a way for teenagers to learn and master skills that are individual and unique to each of us. The field of Academic Life Coaching was born.

Life coaching is the practice of helping others clarify desired outcomes and design systems and habits to achieve them. Academic Life Coaching adds additional tools to this field to help students identify styles of learning and thinking, cultivate talents and passions, and gain skills and experiences to thrive in the future as fulfilled, effective adults.

Over the past eight years, I have worked with over 500 students, amassed over 2,800 hours of individual Academic Life Coaching, and have trained over 1,200 coaches worldwide; from Los Angeles and New York to Johannesburg and Singapore.

I have also had the opportunity to work with faculties from high schools and universities in Canada and the United States, fundamentally changing the approach of schools and educators by equipping teachers and administrators with the tools to support students with a very different kind of skill set.

In his book, *The Element: How Finding Your Passion Changes Everything,* Ken Robinson speaks to the difference between your world, the one with only a single set of footprints, and the outside world in which we all share and interact. In schools and colleges, the shared world outside gets most of our attention. Indeed, the role of a high school teacher or college professor is to teach a group of individuals the same information. It's a process of taking diversity and instilling uniformity. The closer an individual gets to producing one correct answer, the higher the score or grade. Students are motivated and will do almost anything to get a better grade. (Well almost anything if they think it's worth it.)

While contemporary education still follows much of the pattern of the Industrial Revolution's factories, a new kind of work created by the information revolution has created both new challenges and opportunities. With information so readily available, and with the ability to create videos that can be shared across the globe with the ease of pressing a few buttons, education is making leaps and bounds to catch up. The advent of the flipped-classroom, the use of technology and video to deliver instruction, and the unique tech savvy projects that students are creating represent the future of education.

Attending to our individual, internal worlds in a group setting is incredibly challenging. Measuring success is even harder. Yet Academic Life Coaching offers a solution to overcome this challenge. Scholarship such as Christopher Peterson's and Martin Seligman's *Character Strengths and Virtues* and the studies of positive psychology and life coaching are breaking new ground and providing a foundation and vocabulary to help people develop their potential and build on their strengths.

Academic Life Coaching's *1.0 Training Guide* offers a framework for educators and those passionate about education to work with students—and even train students—to develop core internal strengths and virtues that empower them to lead effective, fulfilled lives. The book you are holding in your hands is the roadmap, the foundation for gaining a new set of skills that help students understand their own unique strengths and navigate their internal world. Once students understand their internal world, the external results and successes that are so sought after can naturally fall into place.

I have a few goals for the year 2030. One of those goals is to have an Academic Life Coach in every high school in the United States, as well as in half the high schools throughout the world. Getting help and guidance from an Academic Life Coach will be as accepted as seeking the services of a college counselor.

Based on the growth of the past ten years as well as the data we are getting back from the large number of students with whom we work, I believe the next dozen years is enough time for Academic Life Coaching to find widespread acceptance in schools. If life coaching continues to inspire studies and research that validate its effectiveness and return-on-investment, the next challenge will be to find a way for these concepts to be easily and effectively implemented in schools.

The *1.0 Training Guide* for Academic Life Coaching, which pulls together all the training material for the 24-session Life Coach Training course, is the roadmap and guide to making this goal a reality. It is my sincere hope that you find this training accessible and effective.

Yours in revolutionizing education,

JW

Hood River, Oregon
Updated September 2018

Acknowledgme nts

I would like to thank my Latin students and the clients I have had the honor and pleasure of coaching, and I want to thank Frank Phillips, the principal at St. Mary's School, where I taught Latin and developed the ALC program. Your input in the creation of the *Academic Life Coaching Program* was crucial to both the client workbook and this training guide for coaches.

I also want to acknowledge the coaches who went through the Academic Life Coach Training Program in its early stages. I would like to specifically thank Rawan Albina and Gina Halsted, the first two participants in the ALC program.

I want to thank my former team in Portland, Oregon, Amber Schlossmacher and Emily Adams as well as Janet Birgenheier for her suggestions and edits to the previous edition.

I want to thank Dr. Kathleen Shea Smith from the University of Oklahoma for her support and belief in Academic Life Coaching. Kathleen, you are a force of nature, and we really are revolutionizing the field of education.

To my current team, Ashley Onusic, thank you for your optimism, passion, and energy in holding the team together and moving the vision forward. Rachel Kasperson, thank you for your effort and hard work in keeping the backend organized and the courses running smoothly. And Elle Postel, thank you for your insights and dedication to the mission. You each are an integral part of the team and vision. Thank you.

Thank you too to all the trainers for Coach Training EDU and the Academic Life Coaching Program: Hayden Lee, Lindsay Helm, Bryan Hart, Brittany Barden, Hannah Finrow, Culum Walsh, Teresa Gallis, Michael McBreen, and Amy Gretencort. Our team has never been stronger. Thank you.

I want to give a special thank you to Britt Schlechter for your edits and brilliant insights that went into this edition. Britt, you're amazing. Thank you.

Thank you to my friends who have listened to my ideas about education, business, and life. I would especially like to thank Rajesh Khemraj, Adam Smith, and Tim Saur, my mountain biking buddies, for listening and offering their thoughts on the direction of the book and business.

I would like to thank my two girls, Paloma and Georgiana. This book is dedicated to you. One day, when you are older, I hope you have the opportunity to work with your own Academic Life Coach. (I know I needed an Academic Life Coach when I was a teen.) It is an honor to dedicate this work and this book to you.

And finally, I'd like to thank my wife, Amois, who has been generous and essential to the success of Academic Life Coaching with her support and guidance over the past dozen years. Amois first found life coaching and encouraged me to go into the field. If it were not for her, Academic Life Coaching never would have been created.

With gratitude,
JW

Hood River, Oregon
Updated September 15, 2018

Introduction

As an introduction to Academic Life Coaching, let's explore the theories that have influenced its development. The Academic Life Coaching Program, which includes the training guide you have in hand, as well as the Academic Life Coaching Workbook, relies primarily on life coaching with a theoretical foundation in humanistic and positive psychology. The following outlines the different theories, fields of thought, and models that have most heavily contributed to the creation of the Academic Life Coaching Program.

Behaviorism

In *Behavior of Organisms* (1938), B.F. Skinner laid the foundation for our scientific understanding of habits, habit formation, and habit change. Much like Aristotle pointing to what can be observed, he advocated for a shift away from the "mentalism" of psychotherapy to look again at how elements in the environment shape behavior. He theorized that behaviors were a result of operant conditioning and largely the result of past experiences, current resources, and the surrounding structures.

Why it Matters & How it Applies

Behaviorism points to the importance of a cue in the environment prompting a certain learned action, which ultimately leads to a reward. This cue-action-reward system forms our understanding of habits and provides clues to creating habit change. Habit and behavior change theories can inform coaches on which areas are useful to explore when helping clients identify and change habits. In this training program, you will help students establish well-designed actions and create systems to add structure conducive to behavior change.

Humanistic Psychology

Humanistic studies can be traced back to Socrates and other ancient philosophers. The pursuit of knowledge and understanding of the highest aims of a human being have captured the attention of people for centuries. While the Renaissance led to a revival of the ancient ideas of exploring the human experience and potential, the field arose in psychology in the 1950's in response to psychoanalysis and behaviorism. Humanistic philosophy and psychology posit that everyone inherently wants to do well and that a holistic approach is the best way to address challenges.

One of the most recognized concepts in humanistic psychology is Maslow's hierarchy of needs. Abraham Maslow, in *Motivation and Personality* (1954), theorized that at our core, each of us strives for self-realization: the full realization of our potential to be human. However, such a pursuit requires other needs to be fulfilled before we can fully focus on the next level. He also emphasized the usefulness in shifting focus away from pathology to looking at beneficial traits of being healthy.

In *Emotional Intelligence* (2005), Daniel Goleman outlines five important skills for managing one's own emotions and establishing healthy, strong relationships. Such emotional skills balance the rational stream of thought and can be better indicators of success than results from logic or knowledge acquisition tests.

Why it Matters & How it Applies

Maslow's hierarchy of needs points to the importance of having foundational resources in place to experience higher levels of well-being. He also pointed to the usefulness of exploring "peak experiences" to gain information and insights into an individual's path of self-realization. Self-realization can sometimes be a tricky term and can lead to the idea that a self-realized person has reached some sort of enlightenment or apotheosis. The main idea is that someone at peace with him or herself, as well as with his or her surroundings and situation, will both live a healthy life and do meaningful work in the lives of others.

Goleman's work underlines the importance of the inner work of self-understanding as well as developing stamina and skill to be more empathetic. The Academic Life Coaching Workbook gives students a series of structures that naturally develop emotional intelligence through increased awareness of character traits and developing interpersonal skills.

Positive Psychology: PERMA

Arising out of the trends of behaviorist and humanistic psychology, positive psychology focuses on those elements that lead to well-being. Psychologist Martin Seligman, in *Flourish* (2011), identified five elements of well-being and arranged them in the handy acronym PERMA – Positive emotion, Engagement, Relationships, Meaning, and Achievement. Each element in PERMA is desirable, pursued for its own intrinsic value, and can be measured individually. The PERMA model posits that when all elements are sufficiently present, well-being or flourishing occurs.

Why it Matters & How it Applies

PERMA has been the de facto benchmark and standard of measurement for positive psychology interventions. The elements and scale are also helpful in thinking about the elements that contribute to living a healthy life. The Academic Life Coaching Program directly helps students take concrete action steps in each element of PERMA, creating the conditions of flourishing.

Growth vs. Fixed Mindset

In her book *Mindset: The New Psychology of Success* (2006), psychologist Carol Dweck made an important distinction between two common mindsets based on an individual's perspective on talent and ability. A fixed mindset points to innate talent as the source of ability. Someone with a fixed mindset would agree with the statement, "Everyone has a certain amount of talent" and would agree that a person's level of talent is fixed and that it can only be increased within a certain range. The upside to a fixed mindset is perhaps confidence and a short-term boost in effort. The downside is that a fixed mindset leads to avoiding mistakes at the expense of learning, in a desire to prove talent levels.

A growth mindset points to effort and persistence as the source of ability. Someone with a growth mindset would agree with the statement, "Success depends 1% on talent, 99% on perspiration." The downside of a growth mindset is that it's rare. The upside is that people who have a growth mindset put more attention on effort, developing stamina, and learning from both success and mistakes. Mistakes are seen as an excellent chance to learn. Goals become more about creating a focus point and ensuring continued effort than a way of proving talent.

Why it Matters & How it Applies

Individuals with a growth mindset are more likely than those with a fixed mindset to continue working and putting in effort, even in the face of challenges and setbacks. From the perspective of a growth mindset, talent is simply the starting point and failure and success are just pieces of feedback used to continually improve. While a fixed mindset views maximum potential as measurable and knowable (such as earning a 100% on a test), a growth mindset rejects the idea of a known full potential. From a growth mindset, potential is unknowable and continually increases with feedback and effort. The effectiveness of coaching relies on a coach's ability to help clients shift toward a growth mindset as they take on increasingly challenging goals.

Flow

In his book Flow: *The Psychology of Optimal Experience* (1990), Mihaly Csikszentmihályi describes a state of performance where ability level matches challenge level. It is a state of engagement when someone is immersed in the present moment, completely focused on the task at hand, and performing or working at an optimal level. Focus with a clear goal, instant feedback, and a challenge that pushes a skill set are three of the conditions most conducive to flow. When an individual engages in an activity that pushes the boundaries of his or her performance, skill levels increase. Flow requires ever-increasing challenges to match the ever-increasing skill set. Much like the psychological equivalent of Wolff's Law, which states that the body adapts to the load under which it is placed, someone who experiences flow will adapt to the challenges that are present.

Why it Matters & How it Applies

Flow is often seen as a state of optimal performance, where someone's best work takes place. Understanding the conditions of flow helps individuals design activities and habits conducive to it and build up a stamina for being able to maintain states of flow. Flow can be seen as both aided by the environment or activity, as well as a state that can be developed by an individual regardless of the activity at hand. From a coaching perspective, having clients be able to tap into states of flow while doing useful work is a foundation and recipe for flourishing. In the PERMA model of well-being, flow is accounted for as engagement.

The Academic Life Coaching Program

When a coach uses a coaching approach and the coaching exercises from the Academic Life Coaching Program, students will get to experience elements of these theories. We learn best when we experience the concept directly. When you lean into your coaching skills and allow your client to modify and tailor each of the exercises to him or herself, you empower your client to integrate these concepts into his or her life. Once a client experiences the benefits of the Academic Life Coaching Program, you have helped your client establish a positive spiral of enjoying better external results, while developing more internal capability. Such an upward cycle not only helps clients thrive in the present moment but establish habits and mindsets to enable flourishing throughout their lives.

Chapter 1: Orientation and Foundation

Questions to Consider

Life Coaching

- What are the key mindsets a life coach adopts?

- What is the structure of a classic coaching session?

- In two sentences, how would you describe life coaching?

Structured Improvisation

- Why does more structure allow for more flexibility?

- Why do the basic rules of improvisation work well for coaching?

- What's the relationship between holding a client's agenda and going with it?

- Where in your life have you noticed that you have an easy time going with it?

Levels of Listening

- What is the biggest difference between level 1 and level 2 listening?

- What is challenging about level 2 listening?

Powerful Questions

- What are the criteria for powerful questions?

- Why are simple, curious questions so useful and effective?

- How do you create a simple, curious question?

- What are some of your favorite simple, curious questions?

Life Coaching

life coach |ˈlīf ˌkō ch |

noun
A person who counsels or motivates others in the achievement of personal objectives, such as choosing or changing careers, improving relationships, setting goals, and determining priorities.
DERIVATIVES
life coaching noun

What

Life Coaching is a professional relationship between a client and a coach designed to help the client increase self-awareness, generate learning, and identify and accomplish meaningful goals. The etymology of coach comes from a metaphor of a bus that transports someone to a place he or she wants to go. A coach literally helps people get to their desired goal. It is someone who helps clients determine their next stop and helps them get there. The International Coach Federation (ICF) defines coaching as partnering with clients in a thought-provoking and creative process that inspires them to maximize their personal and professional potential. Here at Coach Training EDU, we like to take this idea of "potential" even further. We like to believe that potential is *unlimited*, thus it cannot be maximized, since maximizing something indicates a limit. We believe that what we are truly capable of is unknown, and we thrive as human beings when we set forth on the journey to discover the magnificence of who we can become and what we can do.

Life coaching helps clients recognize and identify their capabilities and available resources and apply these to their life. Coaching differs from consulting in that a coach does not advise or offer solutions for the client. Coaching differs from therapy in that life coaching does not focus on the past or offer a diagnosis. Coaching differs from mentoring in that mentoring attempts to link someone learning a craft with someone who is already skilled in it. In life coaching, the coach and the client work together to create a deeper awareness and design actions for the client. Coaching focuses on the future that clients want and uses a proactive, forward-thinking approach to help clients get there.

Life coaching is effective for a number of reasons, the primary being that the life coaching relationship is a designed relationship where the coach and the client are equal partners. Such a non-hierarchical relationship provides a foundation for both the client and the coach to explore different areas and be creative in finding individual solutions that work specifically for that client. The coach is not seen as the expert with all the answers. One of the main philosophies of coaching is that the coach trusts that the client already has all the resources within him or herself to be successful.

Life coaching requires three coaching mindsets and seven core-coaching skills, which are detailed below. This "What" section of life coaching also includes a timeline of the classic coaching call.

- **3 Coaching Mindsets.** Life Coaching requires an open and curious mind that avoids judgment and embraces the idea that the client is naturally resourceful. Those ideas play out in the following three coaching mindsets:

    1) **Curious.** Approaching your client with an open mind is essential to being an effective life coach. Open-mindedness and extreme curiosity show up in addressing tough situations without judgment. They lend themselves to a certain mental flexibility that allows for separation from the immediate problem. Such separation allows for an exploration of the client's learning and increases self-awareness. Open-mindedness relies on the next mindset – trusting your client to be resourceful – and shows up as listening with curiosity, not judgment. This mindset is addressed in Training Session 1 with the coaching concepts Curiosity and Powerful Questions.

    2) **Resourceful client.** The second mindset is the assumption you make as a coach that your client is completely resourceful. This assumption helps you avoid going down the rabbit hole of coaching the problem and not the client (which we will explore further in Chapter 3).

    3) **Co-creation.** The third mindset is truly partnering with your client as an equal. It involves co-creating everything from what agenda to address to eliciting insights and

solutions from the client. The opposite would be assuming the role of an expert.

- **7 Core Coaching Skills.** These are the seven skills that you will use during every coaching session you have with a client. We will cover them within the first six training sessions in the 1.0 Academic Life Coach Training Program.

  1) Empathetic Listening (covered in Training Session 1 with Level 2 Listening)

  2) Curious Questions (covered in Training Session 1 with Powerful Questions)

  3) Direct Communication (covered in Training Session 3)

  4) Intuition (covered in Training Session 3)

  5) Addressing Client's Being (covered in Training Session 4)

  6) Addressing Client's Learning (covered in Training Session 5)

  7) Crafting Action and Accountability (covered in Training Session 6)

- **7 Elements of a Classic Coaching Session.** A standard coaching session runs 30 to 60 minutes. It includes these 7 elements:

  1) Connecting

  2) Accountability

  3) Session Agenda

  4) Exploration

  5) New Actions and Accountabilities

  6) Session Agenda Assessment

  7) Logistics for Next Meeting

  Refer to the chart below to see the recommended time spent on each element of a classic coaching session.

7 Elements of a Classic Coaching Session

Element	Approximate length	Description
Connect: Setting the Space	2 minutes	What: Greeting each other and getting connected.
		Why: Establishing a connection sets a safe space conducive to coaching. It also allows clients to clear any distractions, get focused, and be present with the coaching about to begin.
Accountability	About 3 to 7 minutes	What: Asking your client how the previous actions went. Being curious about what your client learned when following through or what changes need to be made to the action.
		Why: Accountability is vital to coaching and making space at the beginning of each call to discuss past agreed upon actions. This gives the coaching a strong frame and sets a good habit for future coaching sessions.
Setting a New Agenda for Current Coaching Session	3 to 5 minutes	What: Exploring with your client what your client wants to receive from the coaching session. The call's agenda is a statement of the new understanding or action steps a client wants to clarify during the present coaching session.
		Why: Having a strong agenda gives the rest of the call focus. It also creates clear criteria for determining the success of the coaching.
Exploring Learning and Being using Coaching Tools	20 to 40 minutes	What: Using the rest of your coaching skills to help your client achieve the call's agenda (what you just co-created) and the larger agenda to help your client thrive.
		Why: Coaching is effective because you are helping your client make important executive decisions on how to spend time and energy, as well as what mindsets are most effective and conducive to living a happy, productive life.
Planning Actions and Accountability	5 to 10 minutes	What: In this part, you help your client design their action steps. Hopefully, an action naturally arose out of the exploration of learning and being questions. If not, you can always simply ask your client, "Out of everything we explored, what action

		steps do you want to take?"
		Why: Action is where the learning and coaching take tangible form. By designing actions together with your client, you empower your client to find solutions, be creative, and become even more energized to accomplish what needs to be done.
Check in on Session Agenda	2 minutes	What: A quick check-in on whether or not you as a coach have successfully addressed the session's agenda.
		Why: Provides accountability for the session and provides a strong beginning and ending structure. Such accountability allows you as a coach to explore tangents, intuitions, and other areas while knowing you will check in again on whether or not you have addressed the original agenda.
Logistics for Next Session	2 minutes	What: A quick conversation about when you will meet next and wishing each other a good week or two.
		Why: Helps cut down on the back-and-forth scheduling process.

Why

Life coaching is effective for several reasons; the most prominent are listed below. The central reason life coaching is effective is because the client is at the center of the process. Everything revolves around the client, and the coach's main role is to focus solely on the client, allowing the coach's natural curiosity to serve the client by exploring areas of a client's life that might otherwise go unnoticed. Here's why life coaching works so well:

- **Addresses executive functioning.** Life coaching is effective because it provides a set time to focus on the client and the client's agenda. It addresses a leverage point of executive functioning: what is most important, what to do next, what perspective to take, how to break up the action steps, what is in the way, what resources are needed, and other higher level thinking. Dedicated time to plan in such a way is rare.

- **Two minds are better than one.** Working with a life coach, clients get twice the brainpower focused on their agenda and life.

- **Coach has a mirror effect.** Sometimes it is a challenge to see ourselves. A coach can help point out blind spots that a client may miss. A trained life coach helps clients see themselves with more clarity and focus.

- **Facilitates effective action.** Goals are great but often create more stress than they resolve. A life coach helps clients design action steps that are more effective and reduce stress.

- **Helps with follow-through.** Accountability is a huge part of what makes a coaching relationship powerful and helps clients follow through on their well-designed actions.

- **Leads to new habits and systems.** In time, effective actions turn into new habits and systems that serve the client. Designing those habits and systems with a coach is a tremendous opportunity to take a struggling area and make it thrive.

- **Results in more fulfillment and meaning.** Working with a life coach helps clients identify and establish action steps based on their values. When clients become more aware of their reasons for acting, they give context to their actions. Such clarity and action result in more fulfillment and meaning.

- **Clients hear themselves say it.** When a client hears him or herself say something that he/she needed to acknowledge, it has a big impact. Oftentimes a client may have been thinking something for a long time, but never had the opportunity to say it out loud to somebody else. A life coach supports the client in breaking down internal resistance and opening new possibilities of action.

- **Solutions are tailored.** A life coach does not focus on "fixing" a situation. Indeed, any solutions created come more from the client than the coach making them perfectly tailored to the situation at hand. Thus, the client is a lot more empowered to follow through on his or her actions and to sustain motivation.

- **Clients get out of their own way.** By identifying and busting limiting beliefs, clients see where they are literally stopping themselves from being successful.

- **Provides a fresh start.** Working with a coach gives clients an opportunity to try something different and open a new chapter in their lives.

How

Learning more about life coaching and getting started on becoming a life coach is an exciting and thrilling process. You do not have to jump in all at once and enroll in the first training program you find. Learning more about life coaching, getting a coach yourself, and taking an introductory course are all great steps to deciding whether being a professional life coach is for you. Here are some recommended steps for learning more about life coaching:

1) **Gather written information.** Gathering written information, like this book and websites dedicated to life coaching, are great starting points and will give you a foundation for learning more about the profession.

2) **Interview life coaches**. Most coaches love the work they do and love talking about coaching. A quick interview can give great insight into what it is like to be a life coach.

3) **Experience life coaching from the client's side.** Hiring your own life coach to experience the process and benefits firsthand is an outstanding way to learn more about coaching.

4) **Enroll in a life coach training program.** Training is essential, and it will take your natural skill set, listening skills, and curiosity to a new level. It is also a great way to start building your support network of other life coaches.

5) **Build your support network.** Starting out as a life coach can be daunting. You can have great conversations with your family and friends to design the best way for them to support you (and for you to give back). Reaching out to other professionals is also an essential part of being a successful and fulfilled professional yourself.

6) **Be kind to yourself.** When starting the coaching process, it helps to be kind to yourself as you climb the learning curve. Coaching is a challenging skill set and process to master, but with practice, you can become a successful life coach.

7) **Get credentialed.** Getting credentialed ensures that you have a core competency in life coaching. The International Coaching Federation (ICF), a non-profit organization and a leader in setting the standards of professional coaching, offers a solid credentialing program. This book is based on the standards and principles outlined by the ICF.

Structured Improvisation

structure |ˈstrək ch ər|

noun
the arrangement of and relations between the parts or elements of something complex.
• a building or other object constructed from several parts.
• the quality of being organized.
ORIGIN late Middle English (denoting the process of building): from Old French, or from Latin structura, from struere 'to build.'

improvise |ˈimprə͵vīz|

verb
create and perform (music, drama, or verse) spontaneously or without preparation.
• produce or make (something) from whatever is available.
ORIGIN early 19th cent.: from French improviser or its source, Italian improvvisare, from improvviso 'extempore,' from Latin improvisus 'unforeseen,' based on provisus, past participle of providere 'make preparation for.'

What

A strong structure (i.e., a clear session agenda, action steps, and accountability) gives you, the coach, increased flexibility to play with ideas, take tangents, and follow your client wherever your clients wants to explore. Such exploration functions like improvisation. Improvisation is the skill of fully partnering with your client to co-create the coaching experience. It requires being comfortable with the unknown and dancing with the unforeseen. It has two primary guidelines:

- Accept what is offered.

- Add value.

The same rules apply in improvisational acting. There is no script, but there is a structure. One of the first rules of improv acting is the "Yes and" rule. In Improv 101, whenever your acting partner offers an idea, you reply with "yes and" and add to the scene.

Life coaching (and life for that matter) operates effectively on those same two guidelines. A coach does not know what is going to happen in any session or how the client is going to be when they show up. However, the coach is open to accept whatever the client offers, and the skill of coaching is to go with it. Such mental flexibility requires you as a coach to be grounded in the present moment and confident that you can dance with whatever comes up. When you learn to trust yourself, your client, and the coaching process, coaching feels easy, effortless, and immensely fulfilling because you know your client is receiving tremendous value.

The opposite of accepting what is offered is called blocking. Blocking denies the client's idea or the premise of the scene. It can be blatant: "Your idea to increase motivation in the office won't work." Or it can be subtle: "I know that you have been putting in a lot of effort to gain this promotion, but stepping up to leadership roles has never been your strong suit." Ouch. Sometimes blocking can hurt.

Accepting versus blocking does not always mean that blocking is bad and accepting is good. Certain situations call for blocking, such as not being on Facebook and finishing employee evaluations instead. However, it is most effective if blocking, or accepting, is used by the coach consciously and for a purpose. Far too often, in a family or business setting, people block out of habit.

In a life coaching session, it is essential for a coach to accept what is offered. Yet, having a structure behind accepting the offer and adding value to it are equally important. The structure behind accepting the offer consists of the coach's ability to hold the focus on the client's agenda, ask powerful questions, and use any other life coaching principles and exercises.

Why

- *Structured Improvisation* **works so well because it mirrors the natural flow of experience.** Something comes up. A coach has a choice to block it and actively work against it. Alternatively, the coach can accept it and use it for future action. Sometimes it is best to block. Other times, it is best to go with what the client wants.

- **Being flexible while having a useful structure is ideal.** The life coaching process contains a balance between flexibility and structure. It is one of the reasons coaching is so effectively employed in a myriad of personal and professional situations.

- **Structure provides freedom.** Having a strong and stable structure, such as the *Academic Life Coaching Program* with its core life coaching principles and exercises, grants the client the freedom to handle more.

- *Structured Improvisation* **leads to changing methods, tools, and systems.** When dealing with stress, most clients rely on the same methods, tools or systems they use every day, trying to convince themselves that they 'just have to try harder.' While this may work at times, it is not the most effective way to solve problems long-term. It would be much more effective for the client to take the time necessary to create new methods, tools, and systems to allow them to sustainably handle more work. This is possible through structured improvisation, a key life coaching principle that forms the structure for clients to handle whatever comes their way in life and work. The stronger the structure, the more the client and coach can handle.

- **Improvisation is unusual in most conversations.** Most people in a conversation are thinking; "How does this apply to me?" It's a perfectly reasonable way to listen to someone and relate to them based on our own experiences. However, in a coaching setting, the coach can accept what the client brings to the session and build from it. When a coach can effectively improvise, it adds so much value to the conversation and works with what the client is already thinking, augmenting it with the coach's natural curiosity.

How

The best way to practice structured improvisation is to practice. Much of the core life coaching principles and Academic Life Coaching class sessions will give you the structure that you need to be a competent and confident coach. The challenge is how to get into the habit of accepting whatever your client brings to the life coaching session.

1) **Accept what your client says.** Judgment gets in the way. Judgement usually comes in two forms: either judging what your client is saying or judging yourself as a coach. This is especially true when coaches judge how well they are doing, how good their questions are, or what value their clients are getting out of the process. Allow your precious focus and energy as a coach to remain completely on your client.

2) **Offer a question based on what you just heard.** A helpful technique is picking out the most interesting word from what your client just said

and building your next curious question around that word. For instance, if we were to pretend that a coaching client said something similar to the paragraph above, we could create a question based on the word "judgment," such as, "What's the impact of judgment in your life?"

3) **Use your curiosity as the structure.** Your natural curiosity will provide a fruitful path forward for your client. You can trust your curiosity – and level two listening – to move your client forward.

4) **Have one of the concepts of the Academic Life Coaching Program in the back of your mind.** It is also effective to build your next question based on one of the concepts in the *Academic Life Coaching Program*. For instance, if you're working through the *Wheel of Life*, you can ask your client about the relationship between two areas on the wheel.

5) **Bounce back and forth between following the client and following the concept.** As you continue to work with your client, *Structured Improvisation* requires bouncing back and forth between following the client on tangents led by your curiosity and using the concepts of the program to inform your intuition on what to ask next.

Levels of Listening

level |ˈlevəl|

noun
1 a position on a real or imaginary scale of amount, quantity, extent, or quality:
a high level of unemployment | debt rose to unprecedented levels.
• a social, moral, or intellectual standard: at six he could play chess at an advanced level.
• a position in a real or notional hierarchy: *a fairly junior level of management.*
ORIGIN Middle English (denoting an instrument to determine whether a surface is horizontal): from Old French *livel*, based on Latin *libella*, diminutive of *libra* *'scales, balance.'*

listen |ˈlisən|

verb [intrans.]
give one's attention to a sound.
• take notice of and act on what someone says; respond to advice or a request.
• make an effort to hear something; be alert and ready to hear something.
ORIGIN Old English hlysnan [pay attention to,] of Germanic origin.

What

The most common distinction made in listening is whether someone is paying attention or not. Listening occurs when someone is hearing the words *and* making sense of them. Paying attention is required to listen, but in life coaching, an important distinction is made by examining the perspective of the coach in attending to the client's words. The perspective the coach takes as a listener has a big impact on the client who is speaking. Those different perspectives make up the three modes of listening:

- **Level One listening is listening for the sake of yourself.** It is necessary and useful when the coach is learning something and needs to know how it applies to his or her own life. When a coach is in Level One listening, he or she is often asking himself or herself the following questions while the client is talking:

    - Is this is really going to be useful for me?

    - Oh, that reminds of me of that time when [fill in the blank].

    - When is it going to be my turn to talk?

    - How does this apply to me?

- I wonder what I could say to look good right now.

- **Level Two listening is listening from the perspective of the person speaking.** It also relates to empathy. Coaches who are skilled at empathetic listening are able to offer their own intuition and curiosity effortlessly for the sake of the client. Still, Level Two listening goes further than just empathy (being able to correctly identify the emotion the client is feeling) to experiencing what the client is saying from her or his point of view. Such deep listening is powerful and moves the coach's interests out of the way. It forces the coach to be much more present and focus on what the client is really saying and feeling.

- **Level Three listening is listening from the perspective of an outside observer looking in on the conversation.** For a coach, listening in Level Three feels as if he or she is standing on the other side of the room, listening in on the coaching session. The coach is listening to the client speaking, listening to the coach's own words, and asking herself or himself questions such as: "How does what is being said relate to my client?" or "If I were an outsider watching this coaching session, what would occur to me?" It is a powerful exercise to help the coach understand that communicating this deeply influences and shapes the conversation. At first, it can seem surreal or artificial. With practice, however, it becomes comfortable for the coach to step outside the conversation, yet be fully present with the client, while simultaneously observing the interaction between coach and client.

Why

Reasons why Level Two and Level Three listening are more effective in coaching than Level One listening:

- **Level One listening is not as effective in serving clients as Levels Two and Three.** People listen in Level One most of the time. However, it can be easy for us to slip naturally into empathetic listening. For example, when a manager and an employee are talking and one is listening deeply to the other, this can move into Level Two listening. This better serves the speaker because it promotes deeper understanding and connection.

- **Level Two listening is a gift to the speaker.** As the coach, keeping your focus on your client's every word allows you to feel like you are in flow, while also gathering the larger meaning and listening between the lines. Such a quality of listening is an acknowledgment that what the client is saying. It is so important that the coach is eager to put 100% of the focus on the client. It is rare in everyday life that clients have somebody dedicated to listening to them with the intention to seek deeper understanding from their point of view. Clients feel heard, which is an incredibly powerful and rewarding experience for them.

- **Level Two listening takes practice and requires focus.** In most life coaching sessions, a coach will primarily be in Level Two listening. Two things often happen when we start coaching. The first is that a coach realizes how challenging it is to stay in Level Two listening. Most coaches tend to think about the next question to ask or become caught up in the client's story and think about a similar story in their own lives. Coaches might also be so concerned with doing the coaching "right" and become more concerned about their performance than the client's experience.

- **Level Two feels good.** The other phenomenon that happens with new coaches is that they will slip into Level Two for an extended period of time. It feels amazing. It feels like they can really understand the client on a deeper level and get lost in the client's words. It is a tremendously creative and fulfilling experience for a coach.

- **Level Three uses a third perspective.** Level Three listening is an important way for the coach to attend to the client-coach relationship. It helps the coach think about the conversation from a different perspective and point of view to make sure that he or she is strengthening the relationship and the professional bond. It is a chance to shift slightly and expand focus to be a more effective listener for the client.

How

An effective coach is self-aware and skilled in choosing the mode of listening that is going to be the most useful to the client.

1) How to listen in Level Two:

- Begin by paying close attention to the words that your client is saying.

- Allow yourself to listen so closely that you could say the same words silently to yourself as your client says them. When you are listening that closely, it feels like an intense form of concentration. Allow your thoughts to center on the client.

- Ask yourself, "How does what this person is saying apply to her or him?" and allow yourself to be curious for the client's sake.

- If you find that you have slipped back into Level One, simply consciously return to Level Two. At times, Level Two listening feels like you are constantly recovering from Level One back to Level Two. Such an experience is okay as long as you remember to recover consistently. Gradually, you will find it easier to be in Level Two with your client for longer periods of time.

2) How to listen in Level Three:

- Begin by listening deeply to your client in Level Two.

- As you are listening, ask about something that you are curious about.

- When your client answers your question, imagine that you are on the other side of the room both listening to the client and watching yourself listen to the client.

- Ask your client another question and try to stay in that third-person point of view. It may feel a lot like mental gymnastics at first, but as you get used to thinking and listening in this way, you will find it incredibly powerful in helping you to listen actively.

Powerful Questions

powerful |ˈpou(-ə)rfəl|

adjective
having great power or strength.
• (of a person, organization, or country) having control and influence over people and events.
• having a strong effect on people's feelings or thoughts.
ORIGIN Middle English : from Anglo-Norman French *poeir*, from an alteration of Latin *posse 'be able.'*

question |ˈkwes ch ən|

noun
a sentence worded or expressed so as to elicit information.
ORIGIN late Middle English : from Old French *question* (noun), *questionner* (verb), from Latin *quaestio(n-)*, from *quaerere 'ask, seek.'*

What

Powerful questions form an essential part of the coaching skill set. Powerful questions are short, direct, open-ended questions that are designed to elicit information from the client and provide insight and learning, as well as motivation, to follow through with action. Powerful questions have the following characteristics in common:

- **Open-ended.** Powerful questions are usually fewer than ten words. They are direct in that they cut to the heart of the matter. In terms of being open-ended, powerful questions usually start with the words "what," "how," "when," "where," "what if," etc. and lead to thought-provoking answers. These contrast with closed-ended questions, which result in "yes" or "no" answers that provide more limited insight. Closed-ended questions typically start with words like "is," "do," "does," "will," "are," "have," etc.

- **Forceful.** Powerful questions also have a certain force about them that make clients want to answer. They are usually questions that may have been roaming around in a client's mind but have not been fully addressed or asked directly. Neither the client nor the coach knows the answer to the question until it is asked, but it is a great question for the client to consider and hear himself or herself answer.

- **More than facts.** Powerful questions are not merely about factual knowledge or information, but rather they address thoughts, habits, and emotions that may not have any known right or wrong answers. When a coach asks a powerful question, the client has an opportunity to deepen learning and to see what is most important to them. It is a chance to try out ideas and see which ones have the most energy or pop. It is also a chance for the client to explore an emotion or use their imagination to conjure up how great it will feel to reach an accomplishment.

- **Based on curiosity.** All powerful questions are based on empathetic curiosity. They are questions that invite the client to become more self-aware and confident about the action that he or she wants to take.

Why

- **Powerful questions give the client space to create a solution.** The ideal solution for a problem comes from the client directly. Sure, general guidelines exist for what constitutes effective time management or the steps in building a successful business. However, the solutions to the deepest problems – and the ones most worth solving – come from within. The force of a powerful question comes from the invitation the coach offers to the client to explore what is really going on from his or her point of view.

- **They are short.** Brevity is beautiful, and it focuses the client's mind on one topic without extra information getting in the way.

- **They inspire creativity.** Most powerful questions start with "what" or "how." Being open-ended allows the client the chance to be creative with the answer and gets the coach out of the client's way. The coach's job is to tap into a client's natural curiosity about herself or himself and point the client in a direction that she or he has not looked before. By asking an open-ended question, the coach stimulates the client's creativity and curiosity to explore and add value to the coaching relationship.

How

Powerful questions require practice. It takes some time to get used to asking a question, then remaining silent to give space for your client to answer. Pay attention to the urge to ask two questions at once, ask a question that is too long, or add a long explanation.

1) First, tap into your natural curiosity, perhaps through Level Two Listening.

2) Start your question with "what," "how," "why," or "what if." "Why" questions can be great, but use them wisely, as it could put your client on the defense. For example, it may be very insightful to ask, "Why is that important to you?" However, asking "Why would you do that?" could cause the client to feel defensive. Instead, try asking, "What reasons led you to do that?" The latter does not question the client's character, but comes from a place of curiosity to learn more about the circumstances of the situation.

3) Keep your question simple and brief.

4) Just ask one question, then stop talking. Pause. Give your client time to think and be introspective. It may feel like an uncomfortably long amount of time, which is okay. From a client's point of view, having that time to think and form thoughts is priceless. Keep in mind that it is likely that your client has never been asked questions like these before, so getting comfortable with silence will be key.

5) Listen empathetically to your client's answer. Repeat steps 1-4.

Examples of Powerful Questions

- What do you want to work on today?

- What is most important to you?

- How important is that to you?

- If you could change just one thing, what would it be?

- What is the biggest change that you need to make in yourself?

- What is the benefit?

- What is the cost?

- Why or why not?

- How do you know it will be successful?

- What happens if you fail?

- What if you knew you would not fail?

- After you accomplish this outcome, what is the next step?

- What stops you from getting what you want?

- What do you need more of in order to achieve your goals?

- What do you need less of in order to achieve your goals?

- What causes you the most fear?

- How does that solution feel?

- How do you know?

- What else?

- Who do you want to become?

- Who do you most admire?

- Why do you want to move forward?

- What values are most important to you?

- What specifically about that value is exciting to you?

- What is your ideal solution?

- What is holding you back?

- How is your action aligning with your intention?

- What is another way to look at this situation?

- What are you learning about yourself?

- What are you learning about the situation?

- What do you hope to learn about yourself?

Chapter 2: Design the Alliance

Questions to Consider

Logistics of a Life Coaching Relationship

- What key factors are foundational to a coaching agreement?

Using the Academic Life Coaching Workbooks

- What is important for a client to understand about coaching and using an outside guide for client sessions?

Design the Alliance

- What is the value in taking time to design an alliance?

- What are the key parts of designing an alliance?

Asking Permission

- Why is asking permission important to life coaching?

- How does asking permission fortify the coach-client relationship?

Bottom-Lining

- What is "bottom lining?"

- When do you ask your client for the bottom line?

- What is the relationship between bottom lining and blocking?

Logistics of a Life Coaching Relationship

logistics |ləˈjistiks; lō-|

plural noun [treated as sing. or pl.]
the detailed coordination of a complex operation involving many people, facilities, or supplies.
• the commercial activity of transporting goods to customers.
ORIGIN late 19th cent. (in the sense [movement and supplying of troops and equipment]): from French *logistique*, from *loger 'lodge.'*

What

Establishing a successful life coaching relationship begins with the first contact between a coach and a client. Establishing the relationship creates the foundation for a professional and successful coaching experience for the client, and is composed of seven parts:

- **Description of life coaching.** The client must have an accurate and complete picture of what life coaching is, as well as expectations of what he or she can expect to get out of it.

- **Limitations of coaching.** It is equally important for the client to understand what life coaching is not. Life coaching is neither consulting nor therapy.

- **Decision of the life coach to work with the client.** For coaching to be successful, the relationship between the coach and the client must be strong. In the back of her or his mind, a coach must be thinking, "Am I a good fit for this client?" If the coach does not believe that she or he is a good fit or good match for this client, then it is a good idea to pass the client on to someone else.

- **Decision of the client to work with the life coach.** The client has an opportunity to evaluate and decide whether he or she wants to work with the coach or not. The client's decision to move forward with the life coaching process is a huge step.

- **Contract.** The life coaching relationship is a professional relationship. Having a clearly defined contract brings a level of professionalism to the practice.

- **Payment.** Payment represents the closed loop in the coach-client relationship. The coach provides the client services, and the coach receives payment for these services.

Why

- **Establishes that the coach is a professional.** It is important for the coach to be viewed as a professional. The performance of a single life coach can form an impression of the profession as a whole. Since life coaching is still a young profession, it is important for life coaches to be mindful of the impact that they have on the profession. The ethical conduct of the coach is the foundation for a successful life coaching practice. You can inform your client that the *Academic Life Coach Training Program* is accredited by the ICF, the highest standard of professional coaching.

- **Frames the work.** Establishing a strong coaching relationship creates the overall frame that will drive all the work that the coach does, even designing the alliance. The initial frame to which a coaching client agrees sets the tone for the rest of the work.

- **Emphasizes the importance of a natural fit.** A coach only wants to work with the clients who are excited to work with him or her. The responsibility of the coach is to find clients with whom he or she loves to work. As they progress, the coach and client realize that magic happens when the coaching is going well. That excitement propels the work forward. When a coach is a good fit with the client, coaching feels natural and easy. It is exciting for the coach to work with clients and deeply fulfilling when the fit is right. A great fit allows both the coach and the client to get the most out of the coaching relationship.

How

1) Begin by establishing a relationship with your client determining what the client is looking for. Ask your client if he or she is familiar with what a professional coach does.

2) Explain the benefits of coaching and the description of what coaching is and what it is not.

3) Offer a free introductory session. Most coaches offer an introductory session that covers a few of the exercises of life coaching and aims to give their client an experience of what it would be like to be coached. It is also an excellent opportunity for the coach and the client to learn more about each other and to get a feel for whether or not there is a good fit. Introductory sessions are an important part of determining compatibility between coach and client.

4) Follow up with the client to discuss starting the coaching.

5) Send a contract to your client and have the client return the contract with payment.

6) Sign the contract and send a copy back to the client. Sometimes it is useful to include an introductory letter or welcome letter to your client.

Using the Academic Life Coaching Workbooks

What once started as a collection of worksheets, the Academic Life Coaching Workbooks leads clients through a set of coaching sessions that introduces young people to the underlying concepts of positive psychology and life coaching. Based on research, as well as feedback and results from thousands of high school and college students, the program is proven to help increase student academic performance, engagement, retention, and overall well-being. It does so by weaving concepts of positive psychology into the exercises in the workbook.

What

- **Thirty-two Concepts.** *The Academic Life Coaching Workbook, High School Edition* covers thirty-two concepts over the course of eleven sessions: one introductory session and ten program sessions. Each of the sessions are designed to take between 30 and 50 minutes. Usually for college students, the number of sessions is lower, and you can choose which exercises fit best to what agenda the student brings.

- **The Introductory Session.** The introductory session, or interview, covers the common myths about coaching, *Core Motivation*, and *Academic Thinking Styles*. It can be found at the beginning of the Academic Life Coaching Workbooks. The purpose of this initial session is to help your client experience Academic Life Coaching and get her or him excited about the rest of the program.

- **Academic Foundation.** The first three coaching sessions focus on designing the alliance between you as a coach and your client, as well as the essential skills, approaches, and motivations to do well academically. Through learning different approaches to studying, creating systems, and discovering new ways to stay motivated, students develop new habits that lead to less stress and better academic performance.

- **Core Coaching Concepts.** The middle section of the program adds support to the new habits and approaches created in earlier coaching sessions. These next sessions address assumptions, perspectives, and values among other typical life coaching tools and approaches. This part of the *Academic Life Coaching Program* is designed to help your client fine-tune and continue to make changes to his or her current systems and habits. It is also useful to lay the foundation for the final portion of the program, which looks toward a student's future.

- **Passion, Projects, and Beyond.** The life of a student is largely future oriented. "What college did you get into?" "What major are you choosing to study?" "What are your next steps to finding a job?" These questions are often on the minds of young people. While traditional education may have given students a foundation to do well on a standardized test, it does not have a reliable mechanism for helping students explore, take chances on developing passions, and be creative in developing skill sets. This section helps a student identify strengths and skill sets he or she wants to develop, and will prompt him or her to create a future plan.

Why

- **Session topics provide structure.** When I was working with high school and college students, I realized very quickly that having a little bit of structure went a long way. An initial structure makes students feel comfortable. Having a workbook establishes the fact that coaching is more about gaining tools and developing positive self-growth, rather than looking to diagnose a complex.

- **Students learn how to use coaching sessions effectively.** Usually by the third or fourth coaching session, a client learns how to use a coaching session effectively. The workbook gives students an initial starting point that the coach can tailor to fit the client's life and situation precisely.

- **The workbook makes the program tangible.** Whether you are delivering the program to college students or giving a presentation to administrators, having a workbook that lays out all of the concepts is a useful tool. It also helps with marketing the program to parents who are wondering what concepts you will cover. There seems to be something about having the weight of a book in your hand when considering the value of a program. Indeed, the word *value* comes from the Latin *valere* meaning *to have worth, to be strong,* and relates to the amount of weight added to scales to determine worth.

How

1) **Develop your approach.** There are two general approaches when looking at delivering the *Academic Life Coaching* program. The first is to follow the session agendas closely, asking clients to use the structure of the workbook to address topics that might fit well with that student. The second is to jump around and use the tool or session that best fits the client's agenda or need for that particular session. I have seen both approaches work well. As you get more comfortable with each of the thirty-two concepts, you will develop your own style in how you use the structure and concepts.

2) **Allow the concept to inform your curiosity.** At the center of being an outstanding life coach is curiosity. Curiosity creates a state of optimal learning and insights in both you as a coach and in your client. The most useful way to approach the concept as a coach is to allow the concept to inform your curiosity. For example, you can use the concepts of conditional and intrinsic motivation to ask questions such as, "How often do you find yourself feeling joy in the middle of solving Math homework?" The question is informed by an understanding of intrinsic motivation and invites the client to explore how he or she experiences little bursts of it in surprising situations.

3) **Use the prompts to refocus a session.** Near the beginning of each coaching session, it is useful - and some could argue essential - to have a clearly defined session agenda. Each coaching session offers its own series of exercises that you can describe in a sentence or two. From there, you can ask your client questions to help define her or his agenda. For example, if you are working with perspectives, you can ask your client about areas where he or she feels it would be useful to

explore different perspectives. You can make establishing an agenda that fits the session topic that easy on yourself and your client. The stronger the session agenda the more ability you have to explore tangents because you can return to a strong structure. You can use the prompts that follow in the workbook to refocus your session and ensure that you are accomplishing what you and your client set out to do.

Design the Alliance

design |dəˈzīn|

noun
1 a plan or drawing produced to show the look and function or workings of a building, garment, or other object before it is built or made.
• the art or action of conceiving of and producing such a plan or drawing.
2 purpose, planning, or intention that exists or is thought to exist behind an action, fact, or material object.
• (often be designed) do or plan (something) with a specific purpose or intention in mind.
ORIGIN late Middle English (as a verb in the sense [to designate]): from Latin *designare 'to designate,'* reinforced by French *désigner*. The noun is via French from Italian.

alliance |əˈlīəns|

noun
a union or association formed for mutual benefit, esp. between countries or organizations.
• a relationship based on an affinity in interests, nature, or qualities.
ORIGIN Middle English : from Old French *aliance*, from *aliere 'to ally'*.

What

The "designed alliance" consists of the details and steps a coach takes to ensure that the client-coach relationship is strong and the environment of each session is comfortable for the client to take risks and be courageous. The basis of creating a "safe space" is that the client-coach alliance is initiated by the coach and designed with the client. The designed alliance is the opportunity for the coach and the client to outline the ways that the coach can best serve the client. These are the elements of a designed alliance:

- **Same page.** The biggest element of a successfully designed alliance is that both the coach and the client are on the same page. Being on the same page does not mean that the coach is the boss or knows more than the client. Being on the same page means that the coach and the client understand three things:

  - Where both the coach and client are in the client-coach relationship

  - Where the client currently is

  - Where the client wants to go and what he or she wants to achieve

- **Confidentiality.** Confidentiality and establishing the professionalism of life coaching is the basis of a designed alliance and a powerful coaching environment.

- **Safe space for ideas and emotion.** Over time, a client learns to trust the coach not just with confidentiality, but also within the coaching relationship, such as when a coach practices *Structured Improvisation* to move the client forward. The client understands that he or she can take bigger risks because the coach's role is not to judge the client, but rather to help the client make progress.

- **Safe space for the actual environment.** The actual environment in which the coaching occurs is an essential element in designing an alliance. A coach must also pay attention to potential distractions and the quality of the environment where the coaching takes place. If the coaching is conducted via telephone or internet, the coach should remind the client that he or she should be in a quiet, safe space free of distractions. (The client should not be driving, looking at other websites, or mutli-tasking while on the coaching call.)

- **Respect and Challenge.** As the coach-client relationship develops, a sense of respect emerges. Such respect demands that coach and client are honest and value the coaching relationship. The coach can also let the client know that he or she may occasionally challenge him or her to think and act in ways outside of his or her comfort zone, interrupt him or her in order to stick to the agenda, and share his or her thoughts and intuitions even if it may not be easy for the client to hear. These risks taken by the coach will be done respectfully with the intention of moving the client forward.

- **Magnificence.** The final piece of the puzzle for a designed alliance is the client's awareness of taking risks and being courageous. When the coach and client establish a strong relationship and space in which the client can take risks, the client's magnificence naturally emerges. The coach is merely a facilitator who sets the stage for the client to perform and discover.

Why

- **Openness**. Rarely are two people so open about how they want a relationship to function. By addressing the relationship itself, coach and client set a precedent for being transparent and open. This openness forms the foundation of trust and allows the client to take risks and be courageous in self-exploration. It also allows the coach to be more confident in providing the client with what she or he most wants and needs.

- **Mutual support.** Like any great team, each teammate needs to support the other players if the team is going to be successful. The chief aim of any designed alliance is to help the client understand his or her role in the client-coach relationship and work to mutually support the coach in designing the best support possible. Coaches find it easy to support their clients. It is a natural byproduct of being a coach. When the client is proactive and understands that he or she also has the power to make the coach more effective, the designed alliance becomes strong. The client understands and takes responsibility for the strength of the relationship. Allowing clients to be proactive in establishing the coaching relationship sets a precedent for them to be proactive in other areas of their lives as well.

- **Freedom from judgment.** Coaching does not assume that something is wrong with the client or that something needs to be fixed. When the client realizes that he or she will not be judged, and the coach-client relationship will not be damaged if the client makes certain requests, then the client learns not to judge herself or himself so harshly. It is incredibly powerful to observe the client and bear witness to her or his growth. It is important to not make judgments, but rather to allow the client to explore areas where he or she can improve. This is a crucial element in a strong and powerfully designed alliance.

- **Coach's skill.** The coach's skill comes into play in the designed alliance and the ability to create a safe space for the coaching to occur. A skilled coach has a certain level of confidence that clients recognize and that provides security.

- **Trained client.** Throughout the coaching process, clients understand the style of their coach as well as the types of questions the coach typically asks. In essence, the client is trained in a deeper understanding of the steps he or she can take between sessions to get the most out of the coaching relationship and what is needed to make the relationship work.

How

Your main objective in the designed alliance is to get on the same page with your client and keep the channel of conversation open about what you can do better. The *Design the Alliance* exercise can be found in Session 2 of the *Academic Life Coaching Workbook, High School Edition.*

1) Start by talking about what an alliance is and what you hope to get out of the exercise (such as being on the same page).

2) Go through the prompts and design your relationship with your client:

   - What best motivates you?

   - How do you move into action?

   - What requests do you have?

   - What do you think I should know?

   - What is working so far?

   - What is not working so far?

   - How will you know that coaching has been successful?

3) After each session, you have the option to write a quick summary to send to the parents or to save in your university's system notes. Such a note helps to keep everyone on the same page. The challenge is to write a note that is informative without sharing something your client would not want someone else to read. You can design the structure with your client and take the last five minutes of each session to craft an email or note to recap the session. Let your client read the note. Ask for suggestions. If there are none, press "send" or "save." The email or note is an excellent way to recap the session and build in accountability for the actions your client agrees to take.

Congratulations! You have just finished your life coaching session.

Asking Permission

permission |pərˈmiSHən|

noun
consent; authorization: they had entered the country without permission | [with infinitive] :
he had received permission to go to Brussels.
• an official document giving authorization: *permissions to reproduce copyright material.*
ORIGIN late Middle English: from Latin *permissio(n-)*, from the verb *permittere 'allow'*

As part of the designed alliance between a coach and client, *Asking Permission* is a crucial skill to establish a true partnership. In the typical flow of a coaching session, the session coaching agenda is set early in the process. After an agenda is set, a coach usually has an idea of what coaching tools to use. Asking permission to use a tool or asking your client which direction he or she wants to take the session nurtures the relationship and cultivates a sense of co-creating the coaching experience.

The Academic Life Coaching Workbooks suggests concepts and exercises in a specific order, and having such a curriculum makes working with students easier. However, asking your client's permission to explore becomes that much more important to ensure that you are still empowering your client with the control over where to take a coaching session. You could say, "I think this is a useful topic to explore, and I have an exercise for values that might work well. Would you like to try it, or perhaps there is another direction you want to explore?"

Asking permission is useful in addressing something personal with your client. It is your acknowledgment and respect for your client's courage and input on which direction to take the coaching session. For example, you could say, "I acknowledge your courage to bring up this topic. Would it be ok if I asked some questions and we coached on it?" Or "Something is occurring to me while you tell your story. May I share it with you?"

Finally, asking permission is helpful in determining which pieces of a coaching conversation you have your client's permission to share and which elements your client wants to keep confidential. The content and description of the elements of the *Academic Life Coaching Program* can be found on the Academic Life Coaching website. Sharing a link with parents about the concepts, while keeping the details of the content of a coaching call confidential, is a great way to keep parents informed yet still preserve coach-client confidentiality. Asking permission is a skill that serves to keep the boundary lines clear and clean.

What

- **Acknowledgment of respect for the client's input.** Asking permission starts with the coach's recognition that the client is talking about a sensitive subject or that you want to try a particular exercise. It emphasizes your partnership with the client.

- **"Yes/no" question.** Asking for permission is usually a "yes/no" question. Unlike the simple, curious questions that coaches ask most of the time, asking permission is an exception to that rule.

- **The client's response.** The client will respond, often saying, "yes," but listen very carefully for any hint of hesitation, emotion, or anything else that seems to come up.

- **Next steps.** If the client wants to continue with the topic or chooses to use the exercise, great. Go for it. If the client hesitates or is unsure, you can ask the client in what direction he or she would like to go or what topic he or she would like to explore.

Why

- **Gives control to the client.** Asking permission is a way for you to partner with your client to co-create the agenda, outcome, and journey of each coaching session. Coaching differs from other practices in that the coach-client relationship is not hierarchical. It is not like a doctor, or consultant, or even a counselor, where the expert has more information or knows more than the client knows. A life coach wants to work as much as possible to be an equal partner with the client. Of course, a coach may have suggestions or insights, but as soon as the coach shares that information, she or he should once again become curious about the client's experience and perspective. While a coach may dip slightly into the role of an expert at times, asking permission is an effective tool to truly partner with clients.

- **Keeps confidentiality.** By asking permission to share with a client's parents, you empower the relationship and design with your client what to keep confidential and what to share.

- **Serves to distinguish different points in a coaching session.** The typical coaching session consists of reviewing accountabilities, establishing an agenda, exploring that agenda, and creating new actions and accountabilities. Asking permission creates smooth transitions from one step to another during coaching sessions.

How

1) Recognize the opportunity to ask permission because the topic is sensitive or you see a need to emphasize your partnership with your client.

2) Ask permission to explore a sensitive topic, use a specific exercise, or go in an entirely different direction.

3) Pay close attention to your client's response.

4) Read the client's response and continue the coaching either along the lines of what you asked permission to explore or ask your client in which direction he or she wants to go.

Bottom Lining

bottom line

noun informal
the final total of an account, balance sheet, or other financial document.
• the ultimate criterion.
• the underlying or ultimate outcome.

What

Bottom Lining is when the coach asks a client to cut a story or an explanation short and identify the main point. It is a way to maintain focus in a coaching session as well as keep the pace of the conversation moving. It usually consists of these parts:

- **An interruption.** *Bottom Lining* is an interruption. Like all interruptions, it can seem rude and clumsy. However, when you recognize that your client is telling a story that is chewing up time more than breaking new ground, it is time to jump in and interrupt.

- **Empathetic listening.** Level Two listening helps make *Bottom Lining* an effective tool. Outside of a coaching conversation, people interrupt each other usually due to boredom or rudeness. However, in a coaching context, when you are listening from the perspective and for the sake of your client, your interruption is in service to your client. Your client will feel the difference. Moreover, listening deeply, even taking time to mirror your client's voice in your head, helps you jump in more naturally and ease the interruption into something useful to your client.

- **Explanation.** If needed, you can explain to your client that you want to interrupt not because you are not enthralled with his or her story, but rather because you want to make the best use of your coaching time together.

- **Refocus on session agenda.** Unlike interruptions in everyday conversation, an interruption by a coach has the purpose of helping move your client forward by refocusing on the client's larger agenda.

Why

- **Provides focus.** Stories and explanations can lead to tangents that take away the focus and the time of a coaching session. Asking for the bottom line preserves focus.

- **Saves time.** Time in a coaching session is precious. As fun as a good story is, serving the client by asking questions that he or she has not considered or pointing him or her in a particular direction will help get to another level. It is a better use of time.

How

1) While listening in Level Two or three, recognize that your client could benefit from cutting the story short and getting to the main point.

2) Interrupt your client. If you feel the need to explain, tell the client that you are interrupting to keep the focus and maintain the pace of the session.

3) Ask her or him to identify the main point.

4) Follow up with a Powerful Question.

Sample Dialogue

Coach: So, now that we got that covered, what do you want focus on next?

Client: I'd like to focus on how I can move my speaking project forward. I wanted to invite a few professional speakers to this event and I'm not sure the best way to do that.

Coach: What was the first thing that came to mind?

Client: Well, I was thinking I could send them an e-mail and explain what we are up to. I know that in the past when I've e-mailed professors it seems to have worked out fairly well. Although the one-time I e-mailed my American Civics professor it didn't go so well. I never really got a response and then when I went into his office and asked him if he got my e-mail, he looked really annoyed with me and it was really awkward. I didn't really feel like it was worth it and looking back on it I shouldn't have been so concerned just about my grade, but rather the class. I mean I liked his class, but-

Coach: What point are you going after?

Client: I guess it's that I think e-mail may be the best way to get in contact, but I'm worried that it won't work.

Coach: Great. Let's address e-mail and contacting these professionals.

The coach and client go on to address the client's *Limiting Belief* around making contact with teachers, e-mail, and being effective.

Chapter 3: Coach the Client, Not the Problem

Questions to Consider

Coach the Client, Not the Problem

- Why is a focus on the client, not the problem, central to life coaching's philosophy?

- What is the downside of a coaching session that focuses only on solving a problem?

- What are a few techniques to keep focus on the client?

Hold the Client's Agenda

- What is the root meaning of the word "agenda?"

- Why are there distinctions among the different kinds of agendas (the client's agenda, the problem's agenda, and the coach's agenda)?

- How does holding the client's agenda set the stage for attending to a client's being, learning, and action?

Direct Communication

- When is direct communication used in a coaching session?

- Why is it important to be bold as a coach?

- How does direct communication benefit a client?

Intuition

- What is intuition; why is it important?

- How do you use intuition in a coaching setting?

- Why is it so important to release your attachment to your intuition being right?

Clearing

- What is "clearing"?

- Why would you use it?

- Why is it important to set a time limit?

Coach the Client, Not the Problem

client |ˈklīənt|

noun
1 a person or organization using the services of a lawyer or other professional person or company
• a person receiving social or medical services.
ORIGIN late Middle English: from Latin *cliens, client-*, variant of *cluens 'heeding,'* from *cluere 'hear or obey.'* The term originally denoted a person under the protection and patronage of another, hence a person "protected" by a legal adviser.

What

At the bedrock of coaching is the concept that the client already has all of the resources that he or she needs to be successful. An effective life coach must approach every client with this in mind and needs to know:

- **The client is not broken.** The coach must take the perspective that the client is not broken, but rather knows the solutions to what is in front of them. It is the coach's job to help them find the motivation to follow through.

- **The difference between creating solutions and fixing problems.** A life coach does not focus on solving a problem or fixing the client. Rather, a coach needs to be more concerned with giving a client the insight and motivation to take powerful action and create lifelong solutions.

- **Clients have the resources.** Coaching assumes that clients have all of the necessary resources that they need to manage their lives and successfully overcome their challenges.

Why

- **This allows the coach to approach the client from an empowering point of view.** A coach is not the expert with all of the solutions, nor does he or she know more than the client knows about his or her own situation. Instead, the coach forms a partnership with the client to help him or her move forward.

- **The coach is a mirror.** The coach becomes a mirror to help the client understand herself or himself and the challenges she or he faces.

- **Assumptions are very powerful.** If the coach assumes that the client cannot do something or that the client needs to be fixed, the coach often comes across as trying to be clever or solve the client's problem.

- **The coach needs to look at who the client is being.** It is important for the coach to look deeply at who the client is being, what perspectives the client is taking, and what is most important to the client. These are the core issues that life coaching addresses. Once these core issues are addressed, all of the other little details (like finding a solution) are much easier.

How

1) First, to understand this concept fully, you must have confidence in yourself and the coaching process. You must also have confidence that your client knows what she or he needs to do to be successful.

2) Ask "powerful questions" and be curious about what your client already knows to help her or him find a solution.

3) Lead your client to have deeper self-awareness and understanding and to hear the solution come out of his or her own mouth. During a coaching session, the most powerful words a client can hear are the words that come from himself or herself.

4) Trust that your client is resourceful. Coaching often feels like a process of recovering confidence in the abilities of your client. Allow the fresh point of view to open possibilities, allow your client to learn more about herself or himself, and pinpoint the obvious solutions for the situation.

Sample Dialogue

Client: I am having a challenging time sitting still in class and staying motivated to take notes. It feels like I don't want to do the work.

Coach: What's stopping you from being motivated?

Client: I don't know. I mean, in some classes I pay attention and the teacher says I do pretty well. But in other classes I just don't care. I think to myself, "What do I need to know this for? There's no point in my life that I will ever need to know this."

Coach: I can imagine it's frustrating.

Client: It's totally frustrating. I know that's part of the cycle.

Coach: So what is it you want?

Client: I think about my classes outside of school and think to myself, "I really don't want to learn this and I really don't want to go to class today." I've had thoughts like that for a long time. It's as if I just forget about all the times that I do want to go to class. I mean, seriously, school is such a drag. I want to go to class and know that the notes I'm taking are going to be useful for getting a good grade.

Current: What is it you're really after?

Client: I want to feel good about myself and I want to feel like I can do this.

Coach: What is it you know you need to do?

Client: I need to sit in the front of the class. Last year I had my stuff together, got good grades, and I definitely sat in the 1st or 2nd row in class. And then I know I got lazy or something, but I just got used to sitting in the back. Maybe the first day it was to just have a break. But I didn't realize that it really does mean something to me to know that learning is helping and to know I can get good grades. It's just something so simple that sitting in the back of class doesn't help and I need to sit in the front of the class.

Coach: What does sitting in the front of a classroom represent to you?

The coaching continues from here and addresses the client's specific action steps. At no point did the coach offer a solution or assume that the client was broken and needed to be fixed. The agenda was clearly set by the client, and the coach used powerful questions to get the client thinking about what was most important. Out of the learning came a natural sense of curiosity, and the client came up with a solution. Ultimately, it helps the client become more confident and learn to align actions, values, and solutions. The solutions are more powerful simply because the client creates them.

Hold the Client's Agenda

agenda |əˈjendə|

noun
a list of items of business to be considered and discussed at a meeting.
• a list or program of things to be done or problems to be addressed.
ORIGIN early 17th cent. (in the sense [things to be done]): from Latin, neuter plural of *agendum*, gerund of *agere 'do.'*

What

The central tenet of successful life coaching is when the coach partners with the client to look at the different areas in a client's life and identify a way to move forward. The client must take full ownership of the coaching session and understand what she or he is gaining from it. Holding the client's agenda involves these four components:

- **Co-design action steps.** The coach helps move the client forward by giving him or her the freedom to stumble upon insights and gain a deeper self-understanding.

- **The coach must set aside her or his own agenda.** Whenever two people sit down to work through a challenge or a problem, there seems to be an impulse for the person who is helping to believe that they have a solution in mind and subtly (or directly) push this solution or agenda onto the other person. It is a natural human impulse to empathize and apply our thoughts to someone else's situation.

- **Serve the client.** A coach needs to be consciously aware that she or he is truly focusing on what is most pressing to the client. By asking the client what agenda he or she has, the client gains control of the conversation, sets the pace, and sets the goals of the coaching work.

- **Keep focused.** Holding the client's agenda also means sharpening the focus by becoming very clear on what it is the client wants and helping the client regain his or her focus when it is lost. The client is able to ramble a bit and go off on a tangent since the coach is present, steadily holding the client's overarching agenda and bringing the client back to focusing on what he or she wants to get out of the coaching. This prevents the coaching session from turning into merely an interesting conversation without any clear focus.

Whose Agenda Are You Addressing?

- **The Coach's Agenda.** This is when the coach is trying to make the session about him or herself. It is usually not intentional, and usually comes in the form of being stuck in one's head, asking the "right" questions, making the session about using a certain tool, doubting if the client is gaining value from the session, or worrying about what the client thinks about him or her as a coach. The Coach's Agenda usually occurs when the coach is in Level One listening.

- **The Problem's Agenda.** This is when the coach makes the session agenda about fixing a specific problem and offering action steps too soon within the session. The Problem's Agenda does not address learning or being and rarely strives to create long-term positive change in the client.

- **The Client's Agenda.** This is the agenda that effective coaches should strive to address. This agenda is about what the client wants, who the client needs to be, what the client needs to learn, and what the client must do in order to achieve what he or she wants.

The Three Parts of a Client's Agenda

1) **The Surface Agenda.** This is the agenda that the client presents and wants to focus on during the session. Often, the Surface Agenda focuses on an action that the client wants to accomplish. This is the default agenda that coaches use at the beginning of the session. The more specific and/or measurable the Surface Agenda is, the more focused and effective the session will be. Coaches often find the session flows better and is more efficient when this agenda is clear.

Sample Surface agenda Questions:

- What specifically do you want to focus on today?

- What result do you want from our time together today?

- How can we measure whether or not we achieved our agenda today?

2) **The Deeper Agenda.** While exploring the surface agenda, the client and coach will often discover that there may be an underlying issue that needs to be addressed in order to fully address the surface agenda. For example, a client's Surface Agenda may be that he or she wants to work on flyers to promote his new fitness business, but the deeper agenda presents itself when the coach and client reveal that he doesn't want his friends to judge him when they see his flyer. The deeper agenda often focuses on who the client needs to be in order to fulfill the surface agenda. In short, most times the surface agenda focuses on an action the client wants to take, and the deeper agenda addresses a change that the client needs to make in himself or herself. Although the deeper agenda is directly applicable to the surface agenda, the deeper agenda can probably be applicable to many areas of the client's life.

   Sample Deeper Agenda Questions:

   - Who do you need to be in order to achieve your agenda?

   - What do you need to change in yourself to achieve your agenda?

   - What strengths and qualities do you need to harness in order to get what you want?

3) **The Bigger Agenda.** This agenda is about the "bigger picture" that reminds the client why the presenting and deeper agendas are important to him or her. The bigger agenda answers the question about the importance of addressing the deeper agenda. It is the "so what?" of the deeper agenda. The bigger agenda could be an overarching theme for all of the work that the coach and client will

do together. In the previous example, the client's surface agenda is that he or she wants to work on flyers to promote his or her new fitness business. The deeper agenda is addressing who he or she needs to be to overcome his or her fear of judgment from friends. The bigger agenda can be that the client is on a mission to share his or her passion for health, fitness, and nutrition to the world in order for others to live longer, happier, and healthier lives.

Sample Bigger Agenda Questions:

- What is the importance of the Surface Agenda and Deeper Agenda to you? (State what those agendas are. It is not necessary to use the terms "presenting" and "deeper", but rather repeat and confirm what the agendas are and ask about their importance.)

- What is the impact on your life if you achieve your agenda?

- What is the impact on your life if you *do not* achieve your agenda?

Why

- **Creates a partnership with the client.** It helps the coach get out of her or his own way and ensures that the client is addressing the desired area of focus. By determining what the client really wants, the coach allows clarity to guide the client's understanding and deepening awareness of what is really important to them.

- **Provides structure to the session.** At times during a coaching session, the conversation can wander between topics, or the client may feel an urge to jump off on a tangent. It's important for the coach to bring the client back to the focus. Holding the client's agenda is a valuable skill that facilitates a focused conversation.

How

1) Ask your client what she or he wants to focus on today. The simple, easy question, "What would you like to focus on today?" works beautifully.

2) Dig a little deeper to get measurable outcomes for the session. Examples are a new perspective, more clarity, two or three action steps, etc. The measurable outcomes are not necessarily fully developed action steps that your client is going to take between now and next session. Rather, the session agenda is the intended purpose of the session to create those action steps.

3) Ask your client what it would mean in her or his life to explore the session agenda and have this agenda go as well as possible.

4) Clarify the session agenda one more time in a yes/no question. "So what you want to explore today is a new approach to exercise and two action steps to take in this next week?"

5) Wait for your client to say a clear and definite "yes." If you client hesitates or wants to change the wording, listen carefully, and repeat the previous step. It may seem redundant or formulaic to say the words back exactly as your client just said them to get a "yes," but it is a useful exercise for you to get on the same page as your client.

6) Ask the client where she or he wants to start. The coaching session is launched! As the session progresses, you will notice opportunities to make the exploration of the agenda more meaningful to your client. In your mind as a coach, you will most likely gain an idea of a larger, or deeper, agenda for your client. For example, the session agenda might be organizing a schedule for the upcoming two weeks. However, a deeper and more meaningful exploration might be the client's relationship with planning and follow through, or perhaps the balance between productivity and procrastination and assumptions about his or her abilities to stay focused and motivated. Such deeper agendas usually point to a client's characteristics, not merely action steps that need to be taken.

7) Tips on how to distinguish among the 3 agendas.

- In general, the "surface agenda" is focused on the short term and an action step (**the doing**). The surface agenda is what is in the forefront of the client's mind, so it usually has to do with something that he or she wants to get done soon. It could also be a current problem that he or she is having and wanting to seek clarity toward finding a solution.

- The "deeper agenda" usually addresses how the client is getting in his or her own way, making it harder to accomplish the surface agenda. In short, the deeper agenda is more about who the client is being and needs to be in order to have more success (**the being**). The deeper agenda of inner qualities that the client is working on (e.g. confidence, trust, patience, self-belief, playfulness, etc.) applies to many areas of his or her life, not just the surface agenda.

- The "bigger agenda" covers the bigger picture, life purpose, and the *why* of what the client does in terms of impacting others and changing the world.

Direct Communication

direct |diˈrekt; dī-|

adjective
extending or moving from one place to another by the shortest way without changing direction or stopping.
• without intervening factors or intermediaries.
• (of a person or their behavior) going straight to the point; frank.
• (of evidence or proof) bearing immediately and unambiguously upon the facts at issue.
ORIGIN late Middle English: from Latin *directus*, past participle of *dirigere*, from *di-* 'distinctly' or *de-* 'down' + *regere* 'put straight.'

communication |kəˌmyoōnəˈkā sh ən|

noun
1 the imparting or exchanging of information or news.
• the successful conveying or sharing of ideas and feelings.
ORIGIN late Middle English : from Old French *comunicacion*, from Latin *communicatio(n-)*, from the verb *communicare* 'to share' (see communicate).

What

Communication is about sharing ideas and information. Direct communication is the skill of being able to clearly communicate and illustrate ideas. Life coaches have the ability to use several tools to communicate directly with clients and provide tremendous value. Direct communication has several different components:

- **Information.** The original idea, emotion, thought, or other information, i.e. message, which a life coach wants to communicate.

- **The sender's intention.** When people are communicating information, there is both the actual message and the intention, or how the sender wants the message to be understood.

- **The method.** The sender has a variety of choices about the method they use to send a message that communicates directly. The next section outlines many of the methods that a life coach could use to communicate directly to the client.

- **The recipient's understanding.** The meaning of the message is some blend of the sender's original thought and what the recipient understands. From the standpoint of life coaching, basing communication on the client's understanding is useful when thinking about developing the method and content of the message.

- **The relationship.** There is always some relationship between the sender and the recipient. The designed relationship of coach and client allows for more direct communication.

- **Directly stating what is currently happening in the session.** Although it can be a risk, a coach can call out a client's behavior during a session, which could lead to further exploration and some great coaching. For example, if a client answers "I don't know" a lot or changes the subject when you try to dig deeper, bring up that observation without judgment and coach away.

Why

- **Clarity.** Direct communication sends a clear message. Such clarity aids a client in cutting through the excuses, limiting beliefs, and worn-out habits to focus on what is truly important.

- **Fine-tuning.** Direct communication is incredibly powerful because a coach in Level Two listening is able to adjust communication for the client's understanding. The coach can ask the client powerful questions to ensure that the message has been understood in a way that aligns with the coach's intentions.

- **Builds the relationship.** From a life coaching standpoint, direct communication is not just communication for the sake of sharing ideas. It also acts as a method for the coach to strengthen the coaching relationship.

How

1) The first step in direct communication is being mindful of both the message you want to communicate and your intention for how you want your client to understand it.

2) Check to make sure you are listening from Level Two.

3) Sometimes direct communication involves taking a bit of risk. Sometimes it does not. The key is to speak clearly and confidently, and cut right to the chase.

4) Closely watch the reaction of your client. A strong life coach maintains awareness of the client's experience.

5) Ask follow-up questions to add value to your client's experience and keep the coaching conversation going.

Intuition

intuition | ˌint(y)oōˈi sh ən|

noun
the ability to understand something immediately, without the need for conscious reasoning.
• a thing that one knows or considers likely from instinctive feeling rather than conscious reasoning.
ORIGIN late Middle English (denoting spiritual insight or immediate spiritual communication): from late Latin *intuitio(n-)*, from Latin *intueri 'consider'* (see intuit).

What

Intuition is a curious thing. When you, as a coach, listen empathetically for lengthy periods of time, you will pick up on certain insights and emotions that may not seem logical. Not only is it important to pay attention to what is being said, but oftentimes it is paying attention to what is *not* being said that can spark your intuition. The skill of intuition is trusting these hunches and sharing them with your client. An important aspect of intuition is sharing in a way that truly serves your client, and does not merely demonstrate how clever or insightful you are as a coach. Intuition plays an important role in a coaching conversation because it expands both coach and client beyond rational, logical thinking. Intuition often opens new paths for the coach and client to travel. Elements of intuition as a life coaching tool include:

- **Insight**. The skill of intuition is based on the coach having an insight that might not make logical sense. It could be an idea that just pops into the coach's head or an emotion the coach is feeling that doesn't quite make sense. For example, you might get the sense that your client is deep down happy that she didn't get accepted to the graduate program, which doesn't make logical sense but opens up other possibilities. Sometimes intuition feels like a whisper. Other times an intuitive hit is loud and proud, and the coach would have to work hard to ignore it.

- **Sharing.** Your intuition only serves the client if you share it. At times, it is useful to preface your intuitive thought. Other times, just jump right in. You can trust the coaching relationship and process.

- **Release**. Not being attached to whether or not your intuition is correct is the most important part of the skill. Even if your hunch is not correct and your client tells you bluntly that in no way does the idea even remotely apply to him or her – you have still moved the coaching conversation forward. If your intuition is off the mark, you might have created more value because you have modeled boldness and risk taking.

- **Curiosity.** Whether your intuition is right on the money or way off base, shifting back to empathetic listening is crucial. Marveling in the magic of your intuition will not serve your client. Wallowing in how wrong your intuitive hit was does not serve the client either. Thinking about how right or wrong your intuition was and making it about yourself is slipping into Level One listening. Get back on that Level Two listening coaching horse, put all your attention on your client, and ask him or her a curious question.

Why

- **Freedom from rationality.** It frees both the coach and the client from the necessity to be logical or for every question to make rational sense. Life does not always make sense, so why should every coaching question be based on rationality or logic?

- **New directions.** Intuition can be a powerful catalyst for a new line of thought to explore. Creating new paths to follow and insights to pursue provides value to your client.

- **Demonstrates failure.** Sometimes it is better for your intuition not to be correct so you can demonstrate elegant failure. If you spectacularly fail, yet recover without blinking an eye, you implicitly give your client permission to take greater risks in the coaching process.

How

1) Begin by actively listening to your client and allow your mind to recognize thoughts that might not make logical sense but may make sense on a different level.

2) Ask yourself if this insight may serve your client or add value to the coaching session.

3) Share the idea with your client and release all expectation of being correct.

4) Ask your client to make it her or his own insight or dismiss it. You can ask questions like:

- I have this idea that [fill in the blank] may be helpful in some way. What do you think about [fill in the blank]?

- If you were to apply [fill in the blank] to yourself, how would you change it to fit perfectly?

- What about this makes sense to you?

- What do you like about it?

- What do you not like about it?

5) Continue to coach. Use curiosity. Ask powerful questions. Finally, allow your insights to add value to your coaching session.

Sample Dialogue

Coach: Now that we've addressed school, let's turn back to what you originally wanted to focus on in the relationship with your family. What would you like your relationship to be like?

Client: I have a pretty good relationship with my dad but I have a hard time with my mom. I like her, but we just don't have that much in common, and it seems like we always get into weird arguments.

Coach: What stops you from avoiding arguments?

Client: She's so…I don't know…it's her comments that just sometimes get me so mad.

Coach: I have a sense that in so many other areas of your life, you have taken control. It seems like here you have gone in the other direction and attempt to take no responsibility or control.

Client: She doesn't understand. She's just so annoying.

Coach: How much control are you giving yourself?

Client: Ok, I know that she says annoying stuff, but I know I also have a role to play too. And I do say some things that I wish I hadn't.

Coach: How would you make the words "taking control" or "responsibility" completely fit your perspective?

Client: What do you mean?

Coach: If you were to use your own words for your part in the relationship, what words would you use?

Client: I would say that I'm not doing much to make the situation better. Yeah, I think it's that I'm not trying to make it better. I'm just allowing it to happen.

Coach: How do you want the situation to change, if at all?

Client: I'd want to take more control of my own responses.

Clearing

clearing |ˈkli(ə)ri ng |

noun
an open space in a forest, esp. one cleared for cultivation.

clear |ˈkli(ə)r|

adjective
free of any obstructions or unwanted objects.
• (of a person) free of something undesirable or unpleasant.
• (of a person's mind) free of something that impairs logical thought.
adverb
so as to be out of the way of or away from.
• so as not to be obstructed or cluttered.
2 with clarity; distinctly.
verb
become free of something that marks, darkens, obstructs, or covers something, in particular
• become free of obstructions.
• gradually go away or disappear.
• (of a person's mind) regain the capacity for logical thought; become free of confusion.
ORIGIN Middle English : from Old French *cler*, from Latin *clarus*.

What

Clearing is a rarely used but valuable tool to have in your toolbox. Sometimes, a client shows up to a session upset about something that just happened. It could be something small, but being upset makes it challenging to focus on what is really important to your client. Some common examples: getting a speeding ticket, finding out about a poor grade, or having an argument with a friend. Clearing is the skill of allowing your client the opportunity to vent the emotion with the intention of getting it out of the way. It helps you and your client focus on a session agenda that really matters. Clearing consists of these five components:

- **Recognition that something is in the way.** It is often obvious when the client has something in the way. A coach practicing Level Two listening can easily tell if the client seems distracted or annoyed by something.

- **Intention to clear.** It is important that the client has a chance to vent feelings of frustration or emotions with the intention to get it out of the way and focus on something else. If the client does not have the intention to move on to what is important, clearing turns into complaining, and there is a danger of the client seeing himself or herself as powerless in the situation.

- **Permission to let it all out.** The coach and the client quickly design the clearing exercise. The coach will underline that the client has permission to let out whatever emotion or frustration she or he has, to get it in the open, and then out of the way.

- **Time limit.** Setting a time limit on clearing helps provide a structure and understanding that there is a definite beginning and end point. In other words, the client has to get down to the "Bottom Line" and get it out of the way.

- **Coach as witness.** The coach's role is to listen empathetically and with the understanding that the client just needs to vent in order to focus on something else. Something may come up and the coach can follow up with powerful questions, but the coach's main role is simply to listen and trust that the client will be prepared to move on to more important work.

Why

Sometimes a client just has to let it all out, and having a trained coach witness his or her emotions and frustrations is a tremendous help. Clearing is effective for the following reasons:

- **Builds the alliance between the client and coach.** Quickly designing the clearing exercise between a coach and client is an opportunity to remind both of the designed alliance and successfully do the exercise with focused intention. Quickly designing parameters of clearing offers both the coach and client the opportunity to revisit the designed alliance.

- **Gets stuff out of the way.** Clearing is effective for helping a client recognize what is in the way and move it aside. It is a great skill to have in a coach's back pocket, especially because the understanding is that whatever is in the way does not necessarily need to be worked out or have an intense focus.

- **Sets a time limit.** The time limit emphasizes the idea that this is something that will eventually end. It empowers the client with the ability to be aware that after venting within the time limit, the focus will shift to something else. It gives the client tremendous self-awareness, allows control over emotions, and provides the client the ability to decide where they ultimately want to focus.

How

1) Recognize that there is something your client needs to clear. It is usually obvious, but sometimes there seems to be something nagging in the back of your client's mind. Trust in your intuition to ask about it as a first step.

2) Briefly explain the exercise of clearing and invite your client to clear.

3) Begin designing the exercise by setting a time limit. Make sure your client knows that your role is simply to witness and listen empathetically.

4) Listen to your client vent emotions and frustration, but keep an eye on the clock.

5) After the time is up, ask your client powerful questions, or give him or her permission to focus on something completely different. At this point, it becomes obvious if your client has really cleared what he or she needs to with the follow-up questions.

Chapter 4: Client's Being

Questions to Consider

Learn-Be-Do Model of Coaching

- What is the Learn-Be-Do Model of coaching?

- Why is it important to include each element in your coaching session?

Client's Being

- What exactly is a client's being?

- Why is focusing on a client's being so important to life coaching?

- What tools help you as a coach address a client's being?

Core Motivation

- Why is core motivation so effective?

- How do you use it in a coaching session?

Learn-Be-Do Model of Coaching

learn |lərn|

verb
1 gain or acquire knowledge of or skill in (something) by study, experience, or being taught
• commit to memory:
• become aware of (something) by information or from observation: [with clause]
ORIGIN Old English *leornian 'learn'* (in Middle English also *'teach'*), of West Germanic origin; related to German *lernen*, also to lore[1].

be |bē|

verb
1 (usu. there is/are) exist
• be present
2 [with adverbial] occur; take place
• stay in the same place or condition
• attend
• come; go; visit
3 [as copular verb] having the state, quality, identity, nature, role, etc., specified:

do|do͞o|

verb
1 [with obj.] perform (an action, the precise nature of which is often unspecified):
• perform (a particular task): *Dad always did the cooking on Sundays.*
• work on (something) to bring it to completion or to a required state:

What

After working with hundreds of clients through thousands of coaching sessions, I found that I was using a very simple model of coaching in my mind. I call it the Learn-Be-Do model of coaching. Often times during a session, a coach is not sure which direction to go. The Learn-Be-Do model is there to guide you. Sometimes clients focus attention on solving a specific problem, and as a coach, it is frustrating trying to get to a deeper level with your client. The Learn-Be-Do model is the map to get to that deep level and do meaningful work that makes a difference to your client.

• **Learn.** Learning is the beginning point of the coaching discussion. As a coach, you are asking yourself what the client is learning about herself or himself. The learning can be focused on the present moment, or it could be a curiosity about what your client wants or needs to learn in the future. Learning is any insight or knowledge your client gains about himself or herself or about a present or future situation.

- **Be.** The second part of the Learn-Be-Do Model of coaching addresses your client's being. This includes attitudes and other personality characteristics, such as perspectives, qualities, habitual patterns of thought, and emotions. You might think of a client's being as his or her personal brand. A brand reflects what your client is all about, core characteristics, and what he or she stands for.

- **Do.** The third part of the model focuses on action. The *do* is your client's action to be completed by a certain time, usually before the next coaching session. By balancing learning and being with action, you ensure that your client is not just spinning his or her wheels, but is moving forward. Action is where learning and being become tangible. A coaching session completes with co-designing the action with your client and addressing accountabilities.

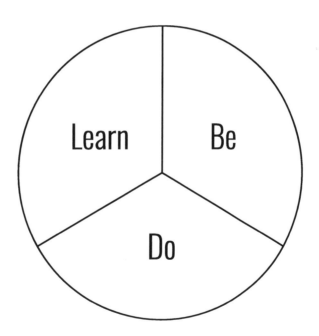

Why

- **It is simple.** The model is simplistic on purpose. When coaching, most of your attention needs to be focused on your client. You need to be listening to what your client is saying, as well as listening between the lines for what your client is not saying. Having the simple model of Learn-Be-Do serves as a guide for your listening and leads to more useful powerful questions.

- **It is complete.** The Learn-Be-Do model covers everything that you need to look at when working with a client. The usual habit of conversation outside of a coaching session tends to focus most attention on action (doing). By taking a step back from such a reflex and putting attention first on learning and being, you help your client create more effective and meaningful actions with a strong foundation of insight and exploration.

- **It includes coaching mindsets.** The model also naturally leads you, as a coach, to include the core coaching mindsets of open-mindedness, client resourcefulness, and co-creation. Because the model is meant to be repeated, learning becomes part of the system as an interwoven and continual exploration. From this perspective, failure is simply more learning to help refine a sense of being and to design new action. By addressing being, you naturally focus on your client. By including doing, you help balance insight with action.

How

1) Start with the Structure of a Classic Coaching Session. Having a strong structure for each call, especially a clear session agenda, helps you be more flexible in your exploration during the session.

2) Attend to the model. Whatever coaching tool you and your client choose to use, make sure that you are asking your client questions that address your client's learning, being, and doing.

3) Repeat.

Client's Being

being | ˈbēi ng |

present participle of be .
noun
1 existence.
• living; being alive.
2 the nature or essence of a person.
verb
1 be present
2 [as copular verb] having the state, quality, identity, nature, role, etc., specified.
ORIGIN Old English *bēon*), an irregular and defective verb, whose full conjugation derives from several originally distinct verbs. The forms *am* and *is* are from an Indo-European root shared by Latin *sum* and *est*. The forms *was* and *were* are from an Indo-European root meaning *'remain.'* The forms *be* and *been* are from an Indo-European root shared by Latin *fui* *'I was,'* *fio* *'I become'* and Greek *phuein* *'bring forth, cause to grow.'* The origin of *are* is uncertain.

What

A discussion on the nature of "being" is beyond the scope of this book. However, life coaching helps the client identify who she or he is being and it is one of the primary reasons why it is so effective. Identities, personality, characteristics, values, thought patterns, and habits all go into how the client views himself or herself and how being shows up in his or her life. Who the client perceives himself or herself to be has a profound influence on the effectiveness of the actions they take and the success experienced in their life.

- **Point to a client's being.** Most goals concentrate on what a client wants to accomplish (the doing). Those are useful goals, but turning attention to who the client wants to become (the being) adds a deeper level of meaning to his or her life. The following kinds of questions point to client's being:

  - What characteristics do you have that you most admire?

  - In accomplishing your goal, who do you want to be?

  - Who do you need to be to accomplish this goal?

  - What does "being a good [fill in the blank] mean to you?

  - When you are at your best, what characteristics do you naturally display?

- What do you think people most admire about you?

- What about yourself do you fear?

- What about yourself do you most admire?

- In your mind, what kind of person is capable of accomplishing this goal?

- **Address the client's being.** There are three factors that help you, as the coach, address the client's being:

  - **Coach's attention.** One of the primary tasks of an effective life coach is to pay attention to who the client is being and how she or he perceives herself or himself. This attention often takes the form of exploring different perspectives and values.

  - **Powerful questions.** Powerful questions are the primary means for a coach to address the characteristics of the client.

  - **Client's awareness.** Responding to a coach's powerful questions, a client develops more self-awareness and deeper self-understanding.

Why

Attending to the client's being is so effective because it helps the client gain clarity about personal characteristics in order to emphasize action that needs to be taken. These are the main reasons why focusing on a client's being is so effective:

- **Fundamental to change.** Often clients are simply not aware enough of themselves or their situation to know what they really want, or to know the true impact that they are having on others or their situation. When a coach brings awareness to who the client wants to be, it is a fundamental step in the process of gaining clarity on what the client really wants.

- **Rare and often the missing piece of the puzzle.** Paying attention to being is rare, yet it is often the piece of the puzzle that allows everything else to fall into place.

- **Slower pace.** Life moves at a rapid pace, and individuals rarely spend time building self-awareness, thinking about what they are learning, and who they are becoming as they take action. When a coach focuses awareness on who the client is being, the coach helps the client understand that who he or she is goes deeper than the actions he or she is taking. When a client slows down the normal pace of life during a coaching session, she or he is able to address who she or he wants to be directly.

- **Fulfillment.** Too often, a client looks for fulfillment outside of himself or herself or wishes the situation were different. Of course, being motivated to make things different is one of the primary drivers for a client to achieve goals and take action. Yet, having a strong sense of awareness is powerful in helping the client appreciate the present moment and the process of achieving a goal, which makes it easier to slip into intrinsic motivation. Addressing the being links a sense of purpose to what the client is doing.

How

The biggest way you help your client become more aware of being is by simply addressing it in your coaching session. Here are some tools that help:

- **Ask powerful questions about who your client is, was, or will be.** When you are stuck on how to incorporate and build self-awareness for your client, asking direct, powerful questions about who your client is or was being helps create self-awareness. Such questions also serve to deepen awareness of what your client is learning about himself or herself, as well as the action that he or she needs to take.

- **Clarify values.** Clarifying values is a powerful exercise for your clients to identify and build on what is most important to them. Chapter 15 takes a deeper look into clarifying values.

- **Acknowledge.** Acknowledgement can be used as a means of articulating what you see as a coach. This helps your client become more self-aware and understand her or his impact more fully.

- **Paraphrase or articulate.** Similar to acknowledgement, paraphrasing what your client just said can serve as a mirror for your client to hear deeper into what he or she has said.

- **Take a bird's eye view.** A bird's eye view helps your client deepen her or his awareness by focusing on the larger picture and what is most important in the long run.

- **Metaphors.** Metaphors are a great tool that can capture the essence of who your client wants to be and the energy she or he wants to emphasize.

- **Direct communication and challenge.** Sometimes a client will state that he or she is already very self-aware of his or her own strengths and weaknesses and knows what needs to be done in order to move closer to their goals. Although the coach will be taking a risk, the coach can then challenge the client by asking what needs to change in him or herself if he or she no longer want to be the kind of person who knows what needs to be done, but doesn't do it. After all, knowledge is not power; implementing knowledge is power.

Core Motivation

motivation |ˌmōtəˈvāSHən|

noun
the reason or reasons one has for acting or behaving in a particular way: *escape can be a strong motivation for travel.*
• the general desire or willingness of someone to do something: *keep staff up to date and maintain interest and motivation.*
DERIVATIVES
motivational |-SHənl| adjective.
motivationally |-SHənl-ē| adverb
ORIGIN late 19th cent.: from motive, reinforced by motivate.

Core Motivation is a personality typing tool used in the introductory interview of the *Academic Life Coaching Program.*

It is based on a personality system called the Enneagram that has been simplified and modified to fit high school and college students. The main purpose of the *Core Motivation* assessment is to raise your client's self-awareness. It also creates insights and opportunities to coach. Landing on the "right" style is not as important as exploring and having fun with the tool. The tool offers coaches an effective map for addressing a client's being and core perspectives on life.

Extremely important to the success of this tool is the mindset that personality is a collection of thought habits and emotions. Like any habit, a pattern of personality can be deeply ingrained and challenging to change. Yet, like all habits, creating change is possible, sometimes even easy, with increased self-awareness and knowledge of how habits work.

The *Core Motivation* typing tool is flexible, allowing clients to be more than one type while acknowledging that we all have aspects of each type in us. By avoiding a dualistic approach to personality – having more of one characteristic means having less of another – clients can capture more accurately the complexities of their unique personality. Someone can be strongly a One and strongly a Seven at the same time.

Approaching the Core Motivation tools with these three points in mind, - emphasis on being, personality as a bundle of habits, and complex flexibility – the coach's job is to raise awareness, explore with the client, then empower the client by following the client's lead on which direction to go with this tool.

What

- **Nine core types.** Core motivation is based on a motivation system that includes nine iconic personality types. Each of these personality types has certain characteristics. Of course, a nine-type personality system cannot capture the complexity of human experience, but the tool still works even if clients identify with more than one type. There is no such thing as a "good," "bad," "right," or "wrong" type. The point is to raise awareness and empower the client with the knowledge and ability to take this tool in whichever direction he or she chooses.

- **Description of strengths.** Each type has certain strengths commonly associated with it. From a strength-finding and coaching perspective, it is extremely useful to build on and cultivate these strengths.

- **Description of weaknesses.** The core motivation tool is both descriptive and prescriptive. It describes each personality's usual blind spots and weaknesses. Sometimes, such raised awareness is enough for clients to make effective change. However, the tool goes one step further. It also prescribes actions and gives suggestions on what can lead to personal growth. Understanding weaknesses and using suggestions offered by the tool can help clients recalibrate the personality's message. This understanding also allows clients to be more thoughtful about the perspectives and actions they choose to adopt.

Why

- **Empowers the client.** A personality system presents the challenge of putting the coach in the role of an expert. Empowering the client, truly partnering with the client through extreme curiosity, and asking permission to explore keeps the coach and client on equal footing. The point of *Core Motivation* is to empower the client with self-awareness and knowledge. As a coach, you use the tool as a starting point to increase empowerment for the benefit of client action.

- **Is easy to use, yet powerful.** When developing the *Academic Life Coaching Program*, we tried numerous personality tools to see which was most effective and useful for students. *Core Motivation* stood out because it is easy to use. A client can often find which one or two types describe himself or herself best in under five minutes. Yet, it is also extremely powerful. Sometimes the insights in those five minutes last a lifetime.

- **Focus on being.** Another challenge of life coaching is addressing a client's being. Using *Core Motivation* helps specifically pinpoint the client's characteristics. It provides a framework to focus on aspects of personality. Like a fish in water, sometimes a perspective or aspect of personality is so close that it can be taken for granted and challenging to describe. *Core Motivation* helps a client gain another perspective on himself or herself, and makes changing personality characteristics less personal and easier to accomplish.

How

1) Have your client read each of the nine paragraphs. Ask him or her to underline sentences that he or she relates to and pick the top two or three paragraphs that fit them best.

2) Become curious about which sentences or aspects of the top choices fit best and why.

3) Choose one or two types to explore in greater depth. Look at the strengths and weaknesses associated with those types. Follow the client's reaction and ideas. Stay curious.

4) Ask your client how he or she wants to use this tool for self-growth.

5) Take the insights gained from the tool and design action that ties back into your client's original agenda for the coaching session.

6) Go over the different *Core Motivation* charts and see what resonates most with your client.

You can use the *Core Motivation* tool throughout the *Academic Life Coaching Program*, not just in the introductory interview. It is presented early in the ALC program so that you can blend its insights into any of the other exercises and tools that follow. At any point in time, you can come back and reference the tool. Ask your client what additional insights he or she has gained after having taken action steps to help cultivate personality strengths and address weaknesses.

Challenges to Personal Growth	Exercises that help Personal Growth
Type 1: The Perfectionist	
Being too hard on myself. Being too serious. Not taking time for myself for fun and pure enjoyment. Demanding perfection and not accepting every part of myself.	Improvisation and activities like improv are outstanding for 1's. Improv activities let 1's act without getting stuck in their thoughts. Taking time out of the day for fun and laughter.
Type 2: The Helper	
Doing so much for others that I forget to take care of my needs. Becoming too involved in relationships. Becoming demanding when I am not recognized.	Write out what you want for each area of your life and determine clearly what balance you want to achieve. Set aside time to treat yourself as you would treat another person.
Type 3: The Doer	
Realizing that your worth is who you are, not what you have accomplished. Sacrificing personal relationships for the sake of a goal.	Relax your focus on success and put your focus on what would fulfill you. Clarify your values and what's really important to you.
Type 4: The Artist	
Over identifying with emotion, especially sad emotion, without moving into action. Resisting change if it is not dramatic. Feeling unworthy. Focusing too much on yourself.	Practice changing perspectives and choosing those perspectives that empower you to get what you really want. Create a positive vision of your future life.

Type 5: The Thinker	
Over-analyzing and being stubborn. Avoiding people or opportunities that seem overwhelming. Being very private. Not moving into action.	Meditation. Especially short meditation during the day to check in with your emotions. When considering an action, go for it.

Type 6: The Friend	
Not trusting yourself or others. Thinking about worst-case scenarios. Wanting to keep knowing more before making a decision. Doubt.	Check in with fear. Practice identifying perspectives and choosing positive ones to move forward. Positive affirmations.

Type 7: The Optimist	
Thinking that something you don't have will be better than what you already have. Avoiding pain and not meeting responsibilities. Being distracted from bigger goals.	Clarify a mission statement and take small action steps to accomplish it. Meditation is very important to 7's. Exercise discipline.

Type 8: The Defender	
Being stubborn. Denying weakness and sensitivity. Fighting any attempt to be controlled and trying to control others. Acting in ways that make success harder to accomplish.	Focus on the gift that you can give to others. Listen closely to others and practice empathy. Resist being stubborn and constantly resisting others.

Type 9: The Peacemaker	
Ignoring problems and trying to be comfortable always. Not meeting problems when they first start and avoiding conflict at any cost. Not knowing what you really want.	Clarify a mission statement and commit to taking small action steps. Practice asserting yourself and saying no to small things. Refuse to be passive aggressive. Instead, be assertive.

Chapter 5: Client's Learning

Questions to Consider

Client's Learning

- What are the three elements of learning?

- How do you focus on a client's learning?

- How does focusing on a client's learning further your client's agenda?

Wheel of Life

- What is the process for creating a *Wheel of Life*?

- What are the benefits of creating and then dating your wheel?

Inquiry

- What is an inquiry?

- Why is it effective?

- When would you usually use it?

Client's Learning

learning |ˈlərni ng |

noun
gain or acquire knowledge of or skill in (something) by study, experience, or being taught.
• commit to memory.
• become aware of (something) by information or from observation.
ORIGIN Old English *leornian* [learn] (in Middle English also [teach]), of West Germanic origin; related to German *lernen*, also to lore.

What

Client's learning is one of the three essential elements of a successful life coaching experience for the client. The other two elements are awareness of the client's being and action with motivation. The client's learning is the knowledge a client is gaining about himself or herself, the situation, and what is possible for him or her. The client's learning occurs both in the coaching session and between coaching sessions. It is facilitated by the coach, but mostly created by the client. A client's learning has three distinct parts:

- **Concept.** Learning happens when a client becomes aware of an idea, emotion, or piece of information. The concept itself is the first part of learning. When people think about learning, most people think solely about the concept.

- **Context.** Learning happens when a concept is placed within a larger context. In life coaching, the client's life is the context in which all other learning takes place.

- **Meaning.** The last piece of learning is the meaning the client becomes aware of when learning a new idea, emotion, or piece of information.

Note: A concept that is placed within a certain context and has a clear meaning encompasses the three essential aspects that make up client's learning.

Why

- **Learning is fun.** The human brain is designed to learn, and learning feels good. Being intrinsically motivated is a wonderful form of sustainable, long-term motivation. It is the way for clients to move forward. Learning about themselves and the world around them helps the clients stay motivated, and creates excitement about the possibilities that lie ahead.

- **Learning fosters growth.** Growing adds a richness to life. When a client is not growing, there is a dullness or listlessness to his or her experiences. Learning is so powerful because it allows the client to continue reaching new levels, helping them continue to grow and stretch in new directions.

- **Opens more possibilities.** Such growth and new directions help clients tap into positive perspectives, which opens up possibilities for more learning and effective action.

- **Gives action another dimension.** In a coaching session, the coach and client will often create action lists. If a coach also checks in with what the client is learning, the coach helps the client add another dimension to the action. The actions become a way for the client to explore and gain more self-awareness and knowledge of his or her world.

How

1) The most important thing to do to help your client develop learning is to be aware of and address the three parts of learning with the client. For example, when you want to lock in your client's learning, the first step is to clearly identify the concept your client is learning. Maintain an awareness that there are many different layers to what is going on. Your ability to distinguish between layers and make distinctions encourages your client's forward motion.

2) The next step is for you to help your client clearly establish the context of the concept she or he has learned. When the context is clear and your client understands that this concept exists within the context, it adds an element of understanding that could otherwise be missing.

3) The third step to lock in learning is helping your client understand the meaning or the reasons behind the concept. Once your client is aware of the reasons for its importance, he or she is taking huge steps towards understanding and learning.

4) The last step is for your client to apply what she or he has learned and move forward. Creating well-designed actions helps your client put the learning into practice.

Introducing a Coaching Tool to your Client

1) Sometimes you will need to introduce a specific tool or concept to your client (e.g. Wheel of Life, Assumption Chart, etc.). Resist "teaching" or over-explaining the concept. Instead, simply remember the three parts of learning by addressing:

  - Concept. What is it? "Here is a tool that will help us today called the Wheel of Life."

  - Context. What is the context? "The Wheel of Life gives us a visual representation of how different areas of your life are doing right now."

  - Meaning. Why is it important? "It helps you quickly assess your levels of satisfaction in different areas of your life and see how they impact each other. It can also give us a good starting point for our coaching conversation today."

2) Jump into the exercise. There is no need to over-explain. This is when you need to trust that the client will understand what you are saying. Trust that if he or she has a question, he or she will ask.

Sample Questions

The following kinds of questions point to a client's learning:

  - What are you learning about yourself?

  - What are you learning about the situation?

  - What do you need to learn in order to accomplish what you want?

  - In what other areas of your life can this learning be applied?

- What did you learn in today's session?

- What has your Future Self learned that you have yet to learn?

Wheel of Life

wheel |(h)wēl|

noun
1 a circular object that revolves on an axle and is fixed below a vehicle or other object to enable it to move easily over the ground.
• a circular object that revolves on an axle and forms part of a machine.
• (the wheel) used in reference to the cycle of a specified condition or set of events.
2 a machine or structure having a wheel as its essential part.
• (the wheel) a steering wheel (used in reference to driving or steering a vehicle or vessel).
• a vessel's propeller or paddle-wheel.
• a device with a revolving disk or drum used in various games of chance.
• a system, or a part of a system, regarded as a relentlessly moving machine.
ORIGIN Old English *hwēol* (noun), of Germanic origin, from an Indo-European root shared by Sanskrit *cakra 'wheel, circle'* and Greek *kuklos 'circle.'*

What

The *Wheel of Life* is a standard life coaching exercise that helps the client develop a snapshot of different areas of her or his life. It invites clients to explore how satisfaction in one area of life may be connected with another. Here are the elements of the *Wheel of Life* exercise:

- **Diagram of a wheel with wedges.** The diagram below is a wheel divided into 8 different wedges. Around each wedge is a label that describes an area of a client's life.

- **Different areas of life.** For students, the different areas are: school, grades, family, friends, health and exercise, fun, cleanliness of their room, and personal growth. The areas for adults are similar except school is replaced with career, grades with finances, room becomes personal space, and you can divide a wedge to add another area.

- **Rating current level of satisfaction.** The coach asks the client to rate his or her current level of satisfaction with each area of life on a scale of one to ten.

- **Follow-up.** Usually a coach will follow up with powerful questions and well-designed actions.

The Wheel

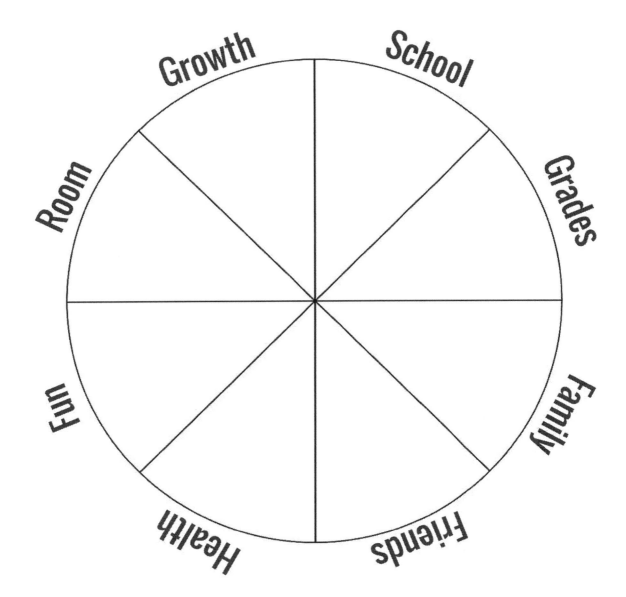

Why

The *Wheel of Life* is a standard life coaching exercise that comes from Neurolinguistic Programming. When using it with teenagers, not much changes except the categories for different areas of life. Throughout the ALC program, you will have your client do four or five wheel exercises, some with variations. The exercise works for the following reasons:

- **Quick assessment.** The *Wheel of Life* offers a quick, subjective assessment of the client's level of satisfaction in different areas. The effectiveness of the tool to quickly uncover different problem areas is immensely helpful.

- **Surprises.** Often a client is surprised that she or he has not considered a certain area of life in some time. The client may realize how that neglect is having a negative influence on her or his life.

- **Connections across areas of life.** The exercise highlights how different areas of our life are connected. If the client improves one area, another area will probably improve as well.

- **Away from "all or nothing" thinking.** The scale of ten helps clients think in terms of elevating their current level of satisfaction by increments, not "all or nothing." Such increments make it easier to create well-designed actions.

- **Easy introduction.** The *Wheel of Life* is an easy introduction to many other areas of life coaching and those that are important to your client. It often leads to solidifying the client's agenda.

How

1) Introduce the concept of the wheel. Identify how it is useful to look at your client's life in defined parts, see the connections, and to address any areas he or she may be neglecting.

2) Draw a circle or use the one on the previous page. As if the circle were apple pie, draw four lines to cut the pie into eight pieces.

3) Help your client create the wheel. Determine the eight areas of your client's life that she or he wants to use. (The wheel shown above was designed for students).

4) Write each label around the outer edge of the wheel:

- School: Overall experience of being in class and working with teachers
- Grades: How happy (or unhappy) the student is with his or her grades
- Family: Immediate family (You may break this wedge into two – parents and siblings.)
- Friends: Quality of relationships with friends
- Health: How healthy the student feels: exercise and diet
- Fun: Time for fun and relaxation
- Room: Degree of cleanliness or messiness of personal space at home (or a dorm room or apartment) and how that feels
- Growth: Degree to which personal and/or spiritual growth is occurring

5) Ask your client to rate his or her current level of satisfaction for each area on a scale of one to ten, ten being the most satisfied.

6) Ask your client powerful questions, such as:

- Looking at your wheel, what jumps out at you?
- If you were to choose just one wedge and take one action to increase that number from a 7 to an 8 (for instance), what would that action be?
- Do you want to follow through with the action? If so, how could we confirm follow-through?

7) In the discussion following the creation of the wheel, make sure to emphasize that the client is simply trying to increase her or his level of satisfaction just one notch higher. One of the biggest assets of the Wheel is helping clients think of incremental improvement rather than trying to go for a 10 or nothing.

8) Create one or two possible actions to take from this exercise and create your client's coaching homework for the session.

9) Save and date the wheels. I do this exercise with myself about once a quarter (every three months), and I date it each time. It is a great exercise to look back and see that the action you take from doing this exercise really makes a difference in your life over the long run. So often successes can get buried in the details of living that we forget how reality looked and felt even three months ago. Consider this an exercise to make sure your client's life is balanced. It is a kick in the pants to get her or him moving, and a tool to remind your client how far she or he has come.

Inquiry

inquiry |inˈkwī(ə)rē|

noun
an act of asking for information.
• an official investigation.
ORIGIN Middle English *enquere* (later *inquere*), from Old French *enquerre*, from a variant of Latin *inquirere*, based on *quaerere* '*seek.*' The spelling with *in-*, influenced by Latin, dates from the 15th cent.

What

- **Powerful question to ponder.** An inquiry is a question designed for the client to ponder. In the context of a coaching session, a coach may leave the client with a powerful question to consider several times between the end of the current session and the beginning of the next.

- **Useful conclusion.** Inquiries are especially useful to quickly conclude a coaching session. For example, imagine you have another appointment coming up in a few minutes, yet the topic and coaching conversation is going really well with no real conclusion in sight. Creating a powerful question for your client to ponder for the next week is a beautiful tool to add value while also concluding a session.

- **Many answers.** Inquiry is not designed to yield one final, definitive answer. Instead, the act of asking the question leads to several different insights and several possible answers depending on circumstances and perspectives. At the next session, picking up on how your client answered the previous session's inquiry is a delightful way to start.

Examples

- Next time you find yourself bored, what are you curious about?

- Who am I now?

- What am I learning about myself now?

- What experiment do I want to try today?

- Why not now?

- At what point in this situation do you trust and release control?

- When working, what distracts you?

- What keeps you focused?

- What do you really want out of this experience?

- Who do you have to be in order to be effective?

- What would being your best self look like this week?

Why

- **Relies on client's strength.** Inquiries are effective because they rely on the client's natural strength to come up with the answers to a question. Inquiries are done best if they are short, open-ended, and designed to help a client approach a situation from many different points of view.

- **Addresses who the client is being.** Inquiries are also useful because they address the client's core beliefs and motivations. Inquiries are often more about who the client is rather than what the client does. Coaching is so effective because the coach looks at both being and doing while reinforcing client learning. The best inquiries include all three: being, learning, and doing.

How

1) First, recognize that your client may benefit from asking himself or herself a question between now and the next session.

2) Ask your client if she or he would like to look at a question between now and the next meeting.

3) Ask two or three powerful questions as the "first draft" of the inquiry. Then, ask your client which question he or she wants to use or if there is anything he or she wants to change about the questions.

4) Make sure you have a clear inquiry.

5) Design how you want to follow up with the inquiry at the next session.

Sample Dialogue

Client: I know that I want to have a great relationship with my teacher, but it's just so frustrating, and I think that talking to her from that point-of-view is hard. I don't like talking to teachers, especially when my grade is so low. It's embarrassing.

Coach: You've got your work cut out for you, but you also have some great tools. I know that you're going to see results. What's the embarrassing part about talking to teachers?

Client: I don't want to be seen as someone who just does something because they want a better grade. I don't want to be a kiss-up.

Coach: That's a pretty negative point-of-view. Based on our work just 20 minutes ago and the perspective that you want to be in, you are clearly motivated not just for the grade but to actually learn the material.

Client: Yeah, of course, but it seems so easy for me to fall back into that kiss-up perspective.

Coach: Oh, wow, we're running short on time. Yet I think there's a lot of juice here for you. Let's get a good inquiry for you to consider this next week and we'll pick it up from there.

Client: Ok.

Coach: How about a question like this, "Who do you want to be as a student?"

Client: [Chuckles] Seriously? That sounds so cheesy.

Coach: What would make it less cheesy and a better fit?

Client: How about, "What kind of student am I?"

Coach: I'm seriously impressed. That's awesome.

Client: Thanks.

Coach: Let's add "being right now." I'd like for the inquiry to have an awareness of the present moment. Let's try "What kind of student am I being right now?"

Client: Works for me.

Chapter 6:
Client's Action

Questions to Consider

Client's Action

- What is the relationship between the client's agenda for the coaching session and the planned action to be taken between coaching sessions?

- What are effective ways for you to co-create a client's action plan?

- If action is central to life coaching, why address it in the ALC training course so late?

Well-designed Actions

- Why do most teens (and people for that matter) get tired of goals?

- Why does creating well-designed actions make more sense?

- What are the criteria for creating a well-designed action?

- What's your favorite of the four criteria? Why?

- For the larger, grand goals that people want to achieve in their life, what's the concept that comes later in the ALC program that best supports people's success?

- How are you going to use the concept of well-designed actions in your life?

- What are the steps in creating a well-designed action?

Brainstorming

- What is so important about splitting the creative and judging process?

- What are you NOT allowed to do when brainstorming?

- What perspective is built into the idea of brainstorming?

Accountability

- What are your thoughts about the relationship between will power, volition, motivation, and follow-through?

- Why is accountability important in a coaching relationship?

- What do you do if your client isn't following through on her or his accountabilities?

Client's Action

action |ˈak sh ən|

noun
1 the fact or process of doing something, typically to achieve an aim.
2 a thing done; an act.
3 [usu. with adj.] a manner or style of doing something.
ORIGIN late Middle English : via Old French from Latin *actio(n-)*, from *agere 'do, act.'*

What

Another key element that makes life coaching so effective is the attention a coach gives to helping a client move into action. Clients come to coaching because they want to achieve certain goals. Coaches help clients gain more clarity about those goals and design an effective plan of action. Helping clients take effective action involves these elements:

- **A clear vision.** A clear vision is a goal, but with more details and a specific time frame.

- **Well-designed actions.** A well-designed action provides clear criteria to ensure that clients take effective action.

- **Alignment with values.** Aligning action with values adds another layer of meaning to those actions.

- **Perspectives.** Perspectives have a profound influence on the success of action taken.

- **Accountability.** Execution and follow-through are just as important as the original plan. Accountability helps keep clients on track.

Why

- **Creates results.** A coaching session is merely a great conversation if afterwards a client does not follow through on the action steps created with the coach. When a client takes action based on a coaching session, it leads to better results through coaching.

- **Incorporates being and learning.** Much of the power of well-designed actions in a coaching session is derived from the incorporation of being and learning into the action.

- **Naturally addresses fulfillment.** Actions taken in alignment with values are a recipe for fulfillment.

- **Forms habits.** Taking effective actions is the first step to developing effective habits.

- **Results are feedback, not judgment.** From the point of view of life coaching, the results from a client's action are merely feedback that provides valuable information for the client and coach. Without the weight of judgment of success or failure, the coach and client can more accurately determine which steps need to be fine-tuned and which steps can be tossed aside completely.

- **Often addresses the leadership element.** When a client takes action, it often impacts more than the client because many well-designed actions involve others. Part of a client's excitement about taking action is the impact that the action has on others from a personal leadership perspective.

How

Many of the following skills and tools directly address helping your client take action. Here are the primary tools and steps:

1) Brainstorm a few possible actions and outcomes that your client wants. Pay attention to those that align with her or his values.

2) Based on the list you and your client create, choose a few to become the framework of a well-designed action.

3) Watch out for negative assumptions and limiting beliefs.

4) Pay attention to perspectives.

5) Discuss accountability to help your client follow through on his or her actions and look at the results as tangible feedback.

Please note: Be mindful if you find yourself jumping to action steps too soon in the session. If this is the case, you may be coaching the problem, and not the client. When a coach starts designing actions toward the beginning of the session, it usually indicates that they have not dug deep enough into the "being" of the client, and are focusing too much on the "doing."

Well-Designed Actions

well |wel|

adverb (better, best)
1 in a good or satisfactory way.
• in a way that is appropriate to the facts or circumstances.
• so as to have a fortunate outcome.
• profitably; advantageously.
2 in a thorough manner.
• to a great extent or degree.

design |dəˈzīn|

noun
1 a plan or drawing produced to show the look and function or workings of a building, garment, or other object before it is built or made.
2 purpose, planning, or intention that exists or is thought to exist behind an action, fact, or material object.
verb [trans.]
decide upon the look and functioning of (a building, garment, or other object), typically by making a detailed drawing of it.
• (often be designed) do or plan (something) with a specific purpose or intention in mind.
ORIGIN late Middle English (as a verb in the sense [to designate]): from Latin *designare 'to designate,'* reinforced by French *désiger*. The noun is via French from Italian.

What

High school students often hear the word "goal." It comes up *all the time*. It comes up at the beginning of the year and when teachers want to motivate their students. It's fine to talk about goals and help students set goals, but for most students, goals just add more stress to the equation. In fact, I'll go so far as to tell students that setting goals isn't that useful. Goals create stress because they usually involve a final outcome that falls outside our control. They tend to be enormous, and are not always measurable. (i.e *I want to be a bazillionaire!*) It is stressful for clients to focus on goals that emphasize how much their fate does not rest in their own hands. *(I want to win the lottery!)* The *Well-Designed Action* is the cure for that problem. It also leads neatly into thinking in terms of systems and the future exercises in the *Academic Life Coaching Workbook*.

Even more fundamentally, goals or grades usually leave the client's habits unchanged. Once a client achieves a goal, he or she usually does not change habits. Continual growth and habit change are what can really make us effective and successful people.

The benefit of the *Well-Designed Action* exercise is that it helps students focus on the actual process that they are going to use to attain their outcome rather than the teleological thinking that setting large goals tends to create. The benefits of having students focus on the process rather than the end goal are:

- Helping them to plan and create a system
- Freeing them up from being stressed out about things they cannot control
- Building self-confidence and increased momentum through a series of little successes

Action is the ability of a client to follow through on ideas. The execution of an idea is more important than the idea itself. Life coaching can take that a step further by asserting that an idea cannot be good unless action is taken.

For the purposes of life coaching, goals and actions will be considered synonymous. Yet, we prefer to use the term "action" because it comes with a fresh context and avoids several of the four common problems with goals:

1) Most focus on the final result and do not address the change in behavior or the action that must also take place.

2) Most have a portion of the goal that is outside the client's control, which leaves the successful accomplishment of the goal up to chance.

3) Most are too vague and not specific enough to sustain motivation and action.

4) When clients get into a goal-setting mode, their goal list seems to get so big that it becomes overwhelming and is soon ignored.

Developing *Well-Designed Actions* avoids these common traps. While setting goals does have some use, focusing on a system or action to achieve it is more powerful and useful for the client. A well-designed action is a clearly defined step worked out between coach and client. While it does not guarantee the client will reach a goal, making a *Well-Designed Action* is the first step in moving towards achieving any goal. A *Well-Designed Action* has these criteria:

- **Is stated in the positive.** A *Well-Designed Action* is something that the client wants to focus on, and focusing on something positive is a great mental habit. It helps clients focus on what they *do* want, not on what they *don't* want. (E.g. Instead of "I won't sleep in," the *Well-Designed Action* would be "I will get up at 7a.m.")

- **Gives the client control.** Getting started and following through with the *Well-Designed Action*, as well as the success (or failure) of the action, depends entirely on the client. The examples provided illustrate the difference between a goal, which involves a portion outside a client's control, and a *Well-Designed Action*, which is totally within the control of the client.

- **Is just the right size.** Usually, goals are huge. Get the promotion. Run a marathon. Buy a first house. Send kids to college. Achieve retirement. Those are great goals, but they are also long-term and too big for a *Well-Designed Action*. A *Well-Designed Action* takes a larger goal, like running a marathon, and breaks it down into many smaller little steps. Each of those steps becomes a separate well-designed action. Two weeks is usually a great action-to-time ratio.

- **Is specific and measurable.** When a *Well-Designed Action* is measurable, it is usually specific as well. Being clear on what constitutes success as well as how you measure success is an important piece of a *Well-Designed Action*.

Examples

Goal: To get all A's.
Well-designed action: To study for all my tests for one hour or more TWO days before the test.

Goal: To not get a bad grade.
Well-designed action: To write in my planner for each class. If I don't have any homework, I'll write "no homework."

Goal: To not be yelled at by my parents.
Well-designed action: To ask my parents to do something fun this weekend.

Why

- **Focus.** Because it is stated in the positive, a *Well-Designed Action* provides a point of focus that is accessible, clear, and moves *towards* what the client wants.

- **Meaning.** A *Well-Designed Action* plays a larger role in a client's overall vision and ultimate goal. Such actions are especially useful because clients can place actions in the larger context of those goals, creating a strong sense of direction and purpose.

- **Control.** Control is often an underrated element in achieving goals. Because so much in a client's life is left up to chance, the biggest virtue of a *Well-Designed Action* is that it empowers the client with full control of the success or failure of the action. For example, it is impossible for a client to control how he or she places in a marathon against competitors. A *Well-Designed Action*, on the other hand, would focus the client on training for the marathon so he or she can do as well as possible. One of most valuable skills people can learn is to turn their attention inward, focus on what they can control in their lives, and follow through on that action. A *Well-Designed Action* helps clients learn—and actively practice—that crucial skill.

- **Habits.** *Well-Designed Actions* are based on changing the actual process the clients use and actions that they take. Over time, changing actions leads to the development of new habits, which makes managing motivation easier and more effective.

- **Small victories.** Because *Well-Designed Actions* most often have short timelines, such as two weeks, they build a certain momentum. Building on the small victories of a *Well-Designed Action* adds fuel for the next milestone.

How

1) Introduce the concept of the *Well-Designed Action* to your client and explain the difference between a goal and an action. Explain how to create a *Well-Designed Action*.

2) Use many examples. I use examples from my own life and from previous clients after I get their permission to share.

3) Brainstorm a list of goals/actions that your client wants in his/her life. Look at your client's *Wheel of Life* to gather information. You can go around the wheel to elicit goals and then convert them into *Well-Designed Action*s.

4) Help your client look at what action she or he can completely control that will most likely lead to achieving the goal.

5) Take a step back and create *Well-Designed Actions* for each of the goals. A *Well-Designed Action* will help your client determine what he or she can and cannot control and will help focus energy on what can be done tangibly.

6) Make sure the actions are stated in the positive. This is usually the easiest change to make.

7) You will most likely have to break apart larger goals and *Well-Designed Actions* into smaller and smaller pieces. Do so. The smaller the time frame, even if it is just for one day, the higher the chances of success and the more likely the client is to see results.

8) Encourage very specific *Well-Designed Actions*, ones that the client can easily measure. The more specific and measurable, the better.

9) Go on to the prompts in this section of the workbook, identifying several well-designed actions.

10) Jumping ahead in the program just a bit, you have a chance to talk about creating a system and *Well-Designed Actions* that can help your client achieve success. *Well-Designed Actions* lead to systematic thinking. Creating systems and using systematic thinking – even just a little bit at this stage – will make the upcoming section on addressing systems and organization, Chapter 10, that much easier.

11) Knowing if your client has successfully followed through on an action is important but is often overlooked. In the workbook, there is a section on identifying what constitutes success. Celebration is a valuable piece in all this, so be sure to emphasize it.

Brainstorming

brainstorm |ˈbrānˌstôrm|

noun
1 a spontaneous group discussion to produce ideas and ways of solving problems.
• a sudden clever idea.
2 a moment in which one is suddenly unable to think clearly or act sensibly.
verb
produce an idea or way of solving a problem by holding a spontaneous group discussion.

What

Brainstorming is the process of generating multiple outcomes, creating a list of options and possible actions, and developing solutions without judging the usefulness of the ideas. The primary purpose of a life coaching session is to get the client thinking about ideas and options that he or she might not have ever considered. Brainstorming is a way of opening-up and discovering more options and opportunities that the client can later explore through actions. Brainstorming has five distinct components:

- **Creativity.** Brainstorming is a process of creating new ideas. Often in life coaching sessions, coach and client will take turns generating ideas. The fundamental basis of any brainstorm activity is that of creation. It is trusting the imagination and letting the imagination flow. Keep in mind this is about generating new ideas, and not about the coach giving the client advice.

- **Absence of judgment; safety to create.** In order for any brainstorming session to be fruitful, it is important to release judgment and not censor new ideas. This is a crucial component because generating ideas only happens in an atmosphere of comfort and safety.

- **Momentum.** A certain flow and momentum is created when coach and client go back and forth in the creation process. That rhythm sets a pace, allows the creativity to flow, and helps both parties refrain from judging the ideas.

- **Excitement.** Brainstorming is fun and creates a level of excitement. This excitement helps move the process forward and aids in momentum.

- **A list.** The end result of a successful brainstorming session is a list of opportunities, ideas, and actions your client can take. This does not mean that the list is inclusive of all of the ideas generated by coach and client. However, it does form a foundation for the client to move forward and design an action based on the newly created list.

Why

- **Safety is created when judgment is placed aside.** Withholding judgment is a key component of brainstorming. It creates a safe atmosphere for the client to generate ideas. That safety is essential and helps strengthen the coach-client relationship.

- **Breaks the creative process into two parts.** Brainstorming is also effective because generally, when ideas are created, there are two steps: the creation of the idea and the judgment of that idea. Those two actions usually occur simultaneously, and sometimes clients even judge the idea before they say it. This does not allow for the free flow of creation. It is crucial for coach and client to approach the creative process in two steps and set aside final judgment of an idea when looking to develop creative solutions and options.

- **Builds on others' ideas.** An important aspect of brainstorming is that it builds on the ideas of other people. An idea generated by either coach or client may spark an idea for the other. Those ideas continue to evolve in the process.

- **Stretches the creativity muscle.** Successful brainstorming stretches that creative muscle. It is an exercise that happens naturally when judgment is withheld. Both stretching the muscle and withholding judgment are part of the same process. In brainstorming, it is a skill that gets better with practice.

- **Taps into a positive mindset of possibility.** The simple act of brainstorming puts both the coach and the client in the mindset that all of these ideas and actions are possible. It happens naturally as a result of working in an atmosphere of safety and delaying judgment. The power of a positive mindset is that it helps clients identify the assumptions they are making. It also helps them discover the many resources they have available, aligning their action with positive assumptions. When action fuses with a positive mindset, it is likely that clients will get the outcomes they desire.

How

1) Recognize good opportunities to brainstorm creative solutions. As a coach, you have an understanding of the different perspectives that your client can use. Know that when you are starting a brainstorming session, you are automatically tapping into a positive perspective that embraces possibilities.

2) Ask your client if he or she wants to brainstorm some possible actions, perspectives, values, or structures.

3) Explain to your client that the process of delaying judgment aids the creative process, and urge him or her to refrain from editing or judging himself or herself.

4) Briefly design with your client how you want to proceed with the brainstorming. Most often coach and client will take turns coming up with ideas. Sometimes the client will get on a roll and throw out several ideas in a row. Sometimes a coach will start with two or three ideas before the client gets warmed up.

5) Brainstorming allows the coach to suggest some ideas that he or she feels may be useful, but the coach must be willing to let go of any ideas that the client does not want to adopt.

6) Start creating ideas. Pay attention to the pace and the tendency to judge the idea as soon as it comes up. As a coach, you can also short-circuit the judgment instinct by generating crazy ideas and keeping the momentum light and free from the inner critic. Demonstrating the free flow of ideas – even if they are silly – will help the client join in the spirit of the brainstorm.

7) Let your client choose the actions, perspectives, structures or ideas she or he wants to embrace.

Sample Dialogue

Client: I can completely see how this last week was so good. I know the next step for me is being able to talk to teachers with more ease and not get so caught up in my grade.

Coach: We've identified some great perspectives. Which one do you want to use this next week?

Client: I really like the "Shiny Chrome" perspective. [The shiny chrome perspective for this client means that he imagines that the homework assignments he has to do have a shiny chrome appearance, with a little sparkle in the corner. It's his perspective that helps him enjoy the actual process of doing the work that he has to do, as well as enjoy the moment when everything is finished and polished like shiny chrome.]

Coach: I think that's a great perspective. Do you want to brainstorm some possible actions that you can create to help remind you of the perspective?

Client: That would be great. How do I start?

Coach: How do you want to start? Usually I find it best if we just trade ideas back and forth.

Client: Sounds good.

Coach: You could get a piece of shiny chrome and put it on your desk.

Client: I love it. That's perfect.

Coach: What's your next idea?

Client: I could get my alarm clock to wake me up in the morning and have its title be "shiny chrome."

Coach: You write out the words "shiny chrome" on your computer and print it out on shiny photo paper.

Client: I could write the words on the outside of my planner.

Coach: After you complete a homework assignment, you could pretend to polish it like it's shiny chrome.

Client: That's awesome.

Coach: Let's keep it going...

Client: After I write an e-mail to my teacher, I could pretend to polish the computer screen.

Coach: You could keep a little a cloth in your pocket and after you create something, you could pretend to polish it.

Client: That's awesome, that's what I want to do.

Coach: We got some great structures to remind you of your perspective.

Accountability

accountable |əˈkountəbəl|

adjective
1 (of a person, organization, or institution) required or expected to justify actions or decisions; responsible.
2 explicable; understandable.

What

Accountability is when a coach checks in on the action that the client decided to take between coaching sessions. As a tool, it helps the coach manage a client's action. From the client's perspective, it can be a powerful tool to keep him or her moving forward on actions. Accountability, at its best, also serves as a structure to measure the effectiveness of a client's action and the systems the client has in place. Here are the components of accountability:

- **Measurable result based on *Well-Designed Actions*.** Accountability has the element of a clear and measurable result.

- **Time set to take the action.** Accountability often includes a plan for when the client is going to take the action.

- **Time set when action is complete.** Accountability includes an end point or a due date for the action.

- **Direct communication.** Accountability includes a time and method for letting the coach know that the action was taken. Usually this is an email, text, or voicemail, although it can be a check-in at the beginning of the next session.

Why

- **Gives structure to action.** Accountability is effective because it serves as a benchmark and a structure for the client to gauge the success (or failure) of an action. It uses *Well-Designed Actions* as a baseline for measurement.

- **Provides feedback on the system.** Systems are crucial to success. Accountability is as much about a client following through on specific actions as paying attention to the learning and effectiveness of a system that is in place.

- **Manages motivation.** The coach's expectation that the action will be completed can be wonderfully motivating for the client.

- **Strengthens the coaching relationship.** Accountabilities are also an opportunity for the coach and the client to redesign their alliance to serve the client better. If a client is having a hard time following through on accountabilities, it is an opportunity for the coach to address this issue in the context of the coaching relationship.

How

1) Help your client come up with a clear goal and establish the next action steps.

2) Determine how your client wants to be held accountable. Does she or he want to email, text, or to check in at the beginning of the next session?

3) As a coach, you also have an accountability to follow up with your client.

Chapter 7: Academic Learning

Questions to Consider

The Science of Learning

- What are the three guidelines to the science of learning?

- What are the three academic thinking styles?

- How do you determine your thinking style?

- Once you have determined a client's thinking style, what do you do with it?

- Why is it important to empower students to engage all the senses?

Acknowledgment

- What is the difference between an acknowledgment and a compliment?

- What is so special about acknowledgment in a life coaching session?

- What would you like to acknowledge about yourself?

Championing

- What is "championing your client?"

- Why is it important to use it consciously and not too often?

The Science of Learning

The Science of Learning is based on three core concepts, with three tools used to support. A major part of the *Academic Life Coaching Program* is helping students become more successful academically. Helping students use the tools below in study sessions is a crucial part of students getting great grades while managing and lowering stress.

What

- **Self-testing.** Self-testing or self-quizzing is a core concept of successful learning. It is the act of creating both questions for and answers to the subject at hand. The *Academic Life Coaching Program* uses the academic thinking styles - what, why, and how - to help students organize thoughts and create mini-quizzes to test knowledge.

- **Increased awareness of memory and thought.** Engaging all of the senses is an important part of learning. The *Academic Life Coaching Program* uses the well-known Visual, Audio, Kinesthetic (VAK) learning/memory styles, but with a twist. Science has debunked the myth that students will learn best if the presented material matches their labeled learning style. However, many students still hang on to the idea of having a primary learning style. The *Academic Life Coaching Program* uses the VAK to guide students to engage *in each of the learning/memory styles*. Engaging as many senses as possible is supported by the science of learning. Using the VAK helps a student avoid the limiting belief that he or she has just one style.

- **Interleaved (AKA spaced) practice.** Intense practice periods interleaved with just enough time for some forgetting to occur is the ideal frequency for long-term learning. Systems and Recipes for Academic Success (in using a planner) address the issue of helping students create interleaved practice. For long-term memory, studying five minutes a day is better than studying an hour once a week.

Why

- **Complete understanding.** The academic thinking styles work because they account for blind spots or sloppy assumptions. Each of the three academic thinking styles - what, why, and how - are necessary to have a full understanding of a topic. Sometimes students assume they know one or two of the other elements. For example, a student primarily concerned with *how* (or steps in the process) might skim over the detailed definition (*what*) or the importance of the concept (*why*). Students who study from all three perspectives ensure a complete understanding of the concept.

- **Structure to test.** The academic thinking styles provide an ideal structure for students to test understanding of a subject. Students have a quick shorthand test by going through the what (names, dates, definitions), the why (reasons and importance), and the how (steps or story) when creating a self-test. Those self-tests increase long-term learning because they force students to use effort to recall information, providing feedback on memory retrieval.

- **Greater awareness.** Both the academic thinking styles and the learning/memory styles (visual, audio, kinesthetic) help create a greater awareness of the internal system of study and memory. By bringing greater awareness, students are then able to adjust the system. More awareness leads to better understanding of what students can change to get better results.

- **Proactive knowledge seeking.** Understanding academic thinking and learning/memory styles also helps students actively seek information. The root of the word *to study* comes from the Latin root *studere,* which means to seek earnestly after something. The contemporary student has seemed to stray far from being an eager and earnest seeker of knowledge, to being simply focused on how to get an A on the next test. Having a structure and more awareness helps students be proactive in seeking knowledge.

- **Brain science of learning.** Having a structure to organize study makes it easier for students to design a way to space study sessions with a concrete goal in mind: do as many reps as possible going through the what/why/how with a visual/audio/kinesthetic cue. The combination of spaced-out study with a proactive, structured learning tool leverages brain science to give a student the best opportunity to discover what study methods work best for him or her.

How: Academic Thinking Styles

As an Academic Life Coach, your task is to raise your client's awareness of thinking styles, and then use coaching skills to design a unique way for your client to apply this to studying. The Academic Thinking Styles exercise can be found in the introductory interview portion of the *Academic Life Coaching Workbook*.

Most students simply review material, perhaps read it over, or do a practice worksheet, and consider it studying. From an Academic Life Coach's perspective, studying is going through each concept and applying the thinking styles to understand it.

The aim of the Academic Thinking Styles exercise is to help students map out and create a system to learn more effectively and efficiently.

1) Introduce the concept of Thinking Styles. It is helpful to give clients a few minutes to read the chapter and the description of each style.

2) Determine your client's thinking style. Explore what your client likes best about learning. When does the concept make sense? What is most satisfying? The details, reasons, steps? Describing each style is usually enough to prime a life coaching conversation on how to best use the styles in your client's learning.

3) Once you have an idea of your client's thinking style, sit with it. Do some coaching around it: "When you write papers for school, do you often find yourself writing a summary?" (Usually a *what* or *how* thinker) "Do your teachers want more examples and specifics?" (Usually a *why* thinker) "Do your teachers want more analysis?" (Typical for *how* thinkers).

4) Look at a passage from your client's textbook. (You can also bring a copy of the PDF *What, Why, How* example of the quadratic equation from the materials page on the Academic Life Coaching website.) Try

to create a few what, why, how notes based on the concept. Ask questions such as: *What* is the concept? *Why* is it important or *why* does it work? *How* do you solve the problem?

5) Design with your client action steps on how to apply the Thinking Styles to notes, studying, and writing.

How: Learning/Memory Styles

The purpose of the Learning/Memory Styles exercise is to help clients learn proactively. It can be found in the *Academic Life Coaching Workbook*. By using the visual, audio, kinesthetic techniques and exercises, you can help your client design a unique system and test how well that system is working. The ideal is for your client to be comfortable adapting to any of the three learning/memory styles and be aware of which style is most useful to them in certain circumstances.

1) Lead students through the learning/memory style quiz and tally up the responses.

2) Don't place too much value on the totals being 100% accurate in determining their style, but use it as a guide to ask questions about learning.

   a. "What style of teaching do you like best? Lecture? PowerPoint? Hands-on projects?"

   b. "If you absolutely needed to get an A on a test, how would you study for it?" (Sometimes it helps draw out a learning style. Sometimes their answer gives you a clue about a learning style that's not working.)

   c. "When you read, do you subvocalize (hear yourself softly say the words in your head), or do you go straight to creating a mental picture?"

   d. "When you spell a word, how do you do it? Do you visualize the word in your mind's eye, then read it? Do you say the letters softly to yourself? Or, is it easiest if you write it down?"

   e. "How easy or hard is it to spell a word forward and backward?"

3) After these questions, the system your client uses to memorize information usually becomes clear. Following the prompts in the workbook to your client's favorite and second favorite style.

4) Design actions, and perhaps small experiments, to help your client explore creating a different system of studying and memorizing information.

Acknowledgment

acknowledgment |akˈnälijmənt|

noun
1 acceptance of the truth or existence of something.
2 the action of expressing or displaying gratitude or appreciation for something.
• the action of showing that one has noticed someone or something.

What

Acknowledgment is when a coach addresses the characteristics or qualities the client drew upon to make something happen, move forward, or grow. It is speaking directly to who the client is. It is pointing out the *being* of the client and putting in the effort to make something happen.

Acknowledgment differs from a compliment in that a compliment usually addresses an action the client has taken, or the *doing*. A compliment, although welcome, usually just skims the surface, while an acknowledgment is a pause in the recognition of something deeper and more permanent. Acknowledgment also differs from championing in that championing points to the potential, or possibilities, for the client if he or she continues to exemplify the qualities that are being acknowledged.

- **Characteristics.** Acknowledgment looks at the specific characteristics of who the client is and the strengths of those characteristics.

- **Heartfelt.** Acknowledgment has a beautiful impact on your client. It communicates connection and caring.

- **Short.** Acknowledgments don't need to be long to be effective. Sometimes the shortest acknowledgments are the most powerful.

Why

- **Points to a deeper truth.** Acknowledgment works so well because it points to something deeper than just the action that the client took. With acknowledgment, the coach addresses who the client needed to be to take that action. Addressing the deeper truth adds power to the coach-client relationship. It encourages the client to look more deeply and fully at herself or himself and assess what she or he is capable of accomplishing.

- **It points to being.** Part of what makes acknowledgment so powerful is that it speaks to the core of a client's characteristics. A coach can point out a positive aspect of a client's personality and draw it out with clarity. It needs to be used carefully, making it one of the reasons why acknowledgment is so effective.

- **Coach has mirror effect.** Clients are sometimes so stuck in the details and the facts of what is in front of them that it is a challenge to see the larger picture, the deeper truth of who they are. Part of the value that the coach brings to a coaching session is the ability to be a mirror and say directly and genuinely what the coach sees.

How

Acknowledgment relies on the coach's ability to remain grounded and listen for the qualities behind their client's success. If your client is describing a story or a particular success/accomplishment, identify what inner qualities were required to achieve that success and spend a few moments speaking to them.

1) While your client is relating his or her specific story/success, listen for the deeper qualities. Identify who your client had to be in order to be successful.

2) Tell your client the specific characteristics you see in him or her, especially those that were required for the achievement.

3) Notice the impact that you have on your client. Follow the acknowledgment with a powerful question.

Sample Dialogue

Coach: Anything else you want to focus on?

Client: You know that brings up something that happened today that was hard for me to do but I did it.

Coach: What happened?

Client: Well, I was invited to a party by a bunch of girls who said they didn't want to invite a different group of girls. I told them it wasn't fair that they weren't inviting the others. They got kind of mad at me and made me feel bad for standing up for those other girls. But I didn't care. I didn't think it was right that they would invite some people but not others. I guess I realized that I didn't want to be friends with those girls if they were exclusive. I just got tired of everything and I finally said something. After, a couple of people came up to me and said they were happy that I said something. The main group of girls said that I wasn't invited either. I totally didn't want to go anyway and told them that.

Coach: It must've been hard standing up to them. What in you gave you the strength?

Client: I felt like I had to defend my other friends. I really did it for them. And a part of it I did for me because I knew that I wanted the group of girls to be more accepting.

Coach: You were courageous. I admire the strength and integrity that you showed. In what other areas of your life can you use that courage?

Client: Definitely talking to my teachers. I know I need to talk with them more, and I do, but I don't let them know how much I don't understand the subject.

The session continued with how the client might apply the characteristic of being courageous to talking to teachers and simply admitting how much she didn't know about the subject.

Championing

champion |ˈchampēən|

noun
a person who fights or argues for a cause or on behalf of someone else.
verb
support the cause of; defend.
ORIGIN Middle English (denoting a fighting man): from Old French, from medieval Latin *campio(n-)* *'fighter,'* from Latin *campus.*

potential |pəˈtenchəl|

adjective
1 having or showing the capacity to become or develop into something in the future .
noun
2 latent qualities or abilities that may be developed and lead to future success or usefulness.
• the possibility of something happening or of someone doing something in the future
ORIGIN late Middle English: from late Latin potentialis, from potentia 'power,' from potent-'being able'. The noun dates from the early 19th century.

What

To "reach one's full potential" may be overused in academic settings, but the meaning is clear: clients have talents and potential for the future that far outpace their current idea of what they think is possible. As a coach, to champion is to help the client cover the gap between her or his current situation and the reality that exists just beyond the next push.

- **Direct statement.** Championing a client means that the coach is directing attention to a client's potential, especially when the client is stuck in self-doubt.

- **A resourceful perspective.** Working with your client from the perspective that he or she has all the inner and outer resources to accomplish the desired outcomes is a fundamental part of being an effective life coach. By adopting such a powerful perspective, your client implicitly (or explicitly if you speak to it during the *Design the Alliance*) adopts the same perspective. Championing serves as a reminder of the resourceful perspective.

- **A coach's trust.** Championing also involves you as a coach completely trusting your client's ability to accomplish the chosen task. Your trust as a coach is an important part of the recipe for what makes championing effective.

Why

- **Coach acts like a mirror.** Sometimes a client has a hard time seeing herself or himself and the potential that is just around the corner. Showing the client how she or he appears to others and what her/his capabilities are is a priceless tool.

- **Exposes limiting beliefs.** In the process of working through several action steps, a client often confronts some limiting beliefs. A coach must pay close attention to the response that the client provides after being championed. Sometimes clients respond with a limiting belief, and it is a wonderful opportunity to expose that limiting belief to help the client move forward.

- **Can serve as a reminder.** At its best, championing acts as a reminder for the client that he or she can achieve desired outcomes. Instead of facing one big insurmountable mountain, the coach helps the client see that the situation is a series of small, but surmountable hills of challenging tasks.

- **Feels great.** It feels great. Having someone champion us feels good. It reminds the client that the coach is someone who believes in her or him.

How

The best championing comes from a genuine vision of who your client is and his or her capabilities. It's a tool that adds strength to your coaching. Powerful questions, risk taking, challenging, and other coaching tools stretch and push your client. Championing gives your client the reassurance that he or she can achieve desired outcomes.

1) Determine where your client needs to go. Recognize that there is a gap in your client's beliefs about herself or himself, self-image, and perception of personal abilities.

2) Gain clarity on the action steps that your client is willing – and wants – to take.

3) Share with your client the strengths, positive characteristics, and capabilities you observe in her or him.

4) Pay close attention to your client's reaction. Listen for any limiting beliefs or signs your words resonated with him or her.

5) Ask a powerful question and continue with the coaching.

Sample Dialogue

Coach: What do you want to focus on today?

Client: The new classes I am starting tomorrow. I was looking at different office supplies this past weekend and was thinking I wanted a completely new and different way of managing my files this semester.

Coach: What kind of filing system do you picture?

Client: I want to find a system that can keep my classes individually filed as well as keeping the most important stuff on top. I know that last semester I had a really good handle on what I needed to do all the time and I really want to improve that.

Coach: What specific things do you want to build on?

Client: I know I was so close to being completely organized last semester, but it seems like in the long run I lose focus somehow.

Coach: The last semester was one of your best. I don't understand why you think you need to revamp your filing system.

Client: I know, I know. Seems like I'm used to freaking out at the start of each semester and thinking that this semester I really need to get my stuff together. I realize that I already have a lot of my stuff together. Okay, I realize I learned how to keep a lot of my stuff together already.

Coach: What's the next step that you're hoping to reach?

Client: I want to be 100% confident in my abilities. I know that putting attention on totally redoing what I did last semester feels like something I've always done year after year, semester after semester, for as long as I can remember.

Coach: I have seen what you accomplished last semester. You merely have to follow through and do what you did just a few months ago. Only this time it is going be much easier because you already have those habits. You've got this.

Client: Thanks. I know. I did really well this past semester and it's unusual for me and I'm not used to it yet.

Coach: It seems to me that instead of completely redoing your systems you can simply refine them. What actions could you take?

Client: I want to get back into some habits for each week. I know it worked really well when I set aside some time every Saturday to look over everything and get ready for the next week. It also works well for me that we have our sessions every Tuesday at 1:30. Also, a couple of my friends talked about working out at the same time every week. All these things would really help.

Coach: Yes, you have this. You're going to get to the next level and this could be even easier than you realize. Let's get clear on your action steps and what you want to produce by next week to keep you on track.

Chapter 8: Making Distinctions

Questions to Consider

Making Distinctions

- What is the process for making distinctions?

- Why is making distinctions important?

- How do you use this concept in a life coaching session?

Bird's Eye View

- What is the "bird's eye view"?

Making Distinctions

distinction |disˈti ng k sh ən|

noun
1 a difference or contrast between similar things or people.
• the separation of things or people into different groups according to their attributes or characteristics.
ORIGIN Middle English (in the sense [subdivision, category]): via Old French from Latin *distinctio(n-)*, from the verb *distinguere* (see distinguish).

What

Making distinctions is a coaching skill that helps clients pull apart two concepts that may be combined together or confused. The art of making a distinction is when the coach is able to notice differentiating details, then pull the concepts into parts that the client can use to make better choices about the concept.

Distinctions are made all the time, and often once a distinction is made, it helps clients better understand habits and thinking. There are two types of distinctions:

- **The first distinction is between what a client is doing and what a client thinks he or she is doing.** Making this distinction can be very important for a coach because it offers clients tremendous value through observations about how the client is impacting other people. This kind of distinction often takes the form of "this is what you think you are doing" versus "this is what you are actually doing" (See the sample dialogue below about reviewing versus studying.) The coach is observing behavior and being a mirror for the client to see himself or herself in a different way.

- **The second distinction is similar, but it has more to do with what the client is thinking or who the client is being.** The distinction can be made between almost any two concepts, such as what is the client doing to act like a good student versus how is the client being a good student.

For example, a client may be really stressed out about earning a bad grade on a final exam. The client is also concerned about the stress of learning the material and making sure that she or he knows the material next year to continue doing well. A coach could help make the distinction between the stress of learning the material well enough to retain it for next year versus the stress of anticipating the final exam grade. By making the distinction, the client can consider the difference in focusing effort on studying rather than on the stress of anticipating the final exam grade

By making the distinction, the coach's curiosity prompts the client to pick apart the difference between being stressed in trying to learn the material versus being stressed to get a good grade. Ironically, the most useful strategy to getting a good grade is to almost forget about the grade and focus on learning the material. Energy spent worrying about the grade is energy misspent.

By making this distinction, the coach may be providing the client with an understanding of what action she or he needs to take as well as shifting the perspective of who she or he is as a student. This provides immense value.

Why

- **Coach is a mirror.** Making distinctions works so well because it is sometimes difficult for clients to see themselves. They often think they are performing in a certain way or doing what needs to be done, but in reality, they are still short of the mark. Such a transmission of understanding goes back to the original meaning of communication: to take an understanding that one person has and make it common between the two. A coach shares an insight that furthers the client's understanding.

- **Unpacks areas of experience.** The concept also works well because clients have many motives, ideas, and solutions wrapped up together. By making distinctions, the coach is helping the client unpack the different areas of experience to deal with them individually. Doing so is often more effective and ultimately more efficient.

- **Promotes deeper understanding.** Making distinctions is a powerful tool and can sometimes be the key that the client needs in order to move forward. Once a coach makes a distinction, it is best to turn the conversation over to the client by asking powerful questions, which promotes deeper understanding of the distinction.

How

1) Recognize the value of the skill and how it will specifically help your client.

2) Explain the difference between the two actions or concepts to your client.

3) It is crucial to ask your client a question that allows him or her the opportunity to incorporate the distinction into his or her perspectives, values, and actions.

Sample Dialogue

Coach: So you want to focus on studying and getting prepared for this next test?

Client: Yes. A chemistry test is coming up and although it is early next week, I know I really want to get studying now but I have so much other work to do and I'm super stressed out.

Coach: If you had an ideal study plan, what would it be?

Client: I would look at the practice problems on the review sheet and I'd study the review by looking it over.

Coach: What is your usual way studying?

Client: Like I said, doing the practice problems and looking over the review sheet to make sure that I understand everything.

Coach: What's the difference between studying and reviewing? [The coach is making a distinction here in the form of a question]

Client: Well, studying is going over the review sheet.

Coach: It seems to me there's a difference between looking over something as a review versus actively studying and making sure you can identify the concepts and how they fit together. If you make a distinction between studying and reviewing what would that distinction be?

Client: You know, I often think of studying and reviewing as the same thing, but if I were to look at them differently I think what I've been doing is reviewing. I know that when I go through the chapter and make my own review sheet I do better. But that takes more time, and I'm already pressed for time.

Coach: How much time does it take?

Client: Yeah ok, now I'm realizing that it takes way more effort to go through my notes and make my own review sheet—but I'm thinking back to the third chapter when I did that and I got a 91% on the test. It felt soooooo good.

Coach: Worth it?

Client: For sure.

Coach: What's the next step?

Bird's Eye View

bird's eye view

noun
a general view from above.
• a general view as if from above : the map gives a bird's-eye view of the route.
• a broad or general consideration of something.

view |vyoō|

noun
1 the ability to see something or to be seen from a particular place.
• the visual appearance or an image of something when looked at in a particular way.
2 a particular way of considering or regarding something; an attitude or opinion.
verb
1 look at or inspect something.
2 regard in a particular light or with a particular attitude.
ORIGIN Middle English : from Anglo-Norman French *vieue*, feminine past participle of *veoir 'see,'* from Latin *videre*. The verb dates from the early 16th cent.

What

- **Big picture perspective.** The "Bird's Eye View" is the act of pulling the client's perspective up into the sky and taking a look at the situation from farther away. Essentially, it is a pre-determined, bigger picture perspective.

- **Reset button.** Sometimes in a coaching session, a client can get caught up in details of a story or a certain perspective can sink in. The Bird's Eye View acts like a reset button during a coaching session, helping both you and your client take a step back to reevaluate the progress made and choose a new direction to take.

Why

- **Provides clarity.** Sometimes, when a client is so tied up in irrelevant details, pulling back and getting a larger picture perspective shines a light on what is important.

- **Speeds up the process.** The bird's eye view is a ready-made perspective. A coach or client does not have to go through the whole process of generating different perspectives.

- **Allows change-up.** If a coach does not know where to go with the next question, a change-up is always useful. The bird's eye view is an effective change-up and often provides insight into where to take the coaching session.

How

1) Recognize the value of the bird's eye view and decide that now would be a great time to pull back and ask questions from a larger perspective. It is especially useful if you feel the client is constricted or tied up in details.

2) Direct your client to take a bird's eye view. "For a moment, let's take a bird's eye view. If you were to look down on this situation from far up in the sky, what would occur to you?"

3) Be in Level Two listening. Then take the coaching conversation wherever your client needs to go next.

Sample Dialogue

Client: Sometimes I get so frustrated with grades and I don't really know what I could do different.

Coach: What's the ideal?

Client: Getting all A's and B's.

Coach: What stops you?

Client: I get too tied up in everything. My mom can't pick me up until 5 so I stay at school. I have soccer from 7 to 9 most nights, which doesn't give me a lot of time to do my school work. And then from after school to 5, I have conditioning and take a break to hang out with my friends. It's like this every week. I know that I could do more school work, but I feel like I'm bouncing around from activity to activity trying to keep track of all these assignments and then when I start I'm exhausted.

Coach: Maybe we can look at this from a longer-range perspective. If you were way up high looking down on the situation and saw yourself go through this same process day after day, what occurs to you?

Client: That I'm continually tired. I never really get a break, and then on the weekends.... I guess I crash. It's like I spend all week going as fast as I can and then do nothing on the weekends until Sunday night.

Coach: What do you want to change?

Client: If I could do just a little more work on Sunday, start earlier rather than 8 or 9 when I start to feel stressed out, that would really help.

Chapter 9: Vision

Questions to Consider

Vision

- What are the differences between well-designed actions, goals, and vision?

- Why is having a structure to remind you of that vision crucial?

- What are the elements of a useful structure?

Vision Recording

- What is a vision recording?

- Why is it effective?

Metaphor

- When do you use metaphor?

- What are the benefits of using a metaphor?

Challenge

- When do you use challenge?

- Why does challenging your client work?

Vision

vision |ˈvi zh ən|

noun
the faculty or state of being able to see.
• the ability to think about or plan the future with imagination or wisdom.
• a mental image of what the future will or could be like.
ORIGIN Middle English (denoting a supernatural apparition): via Old French from Latin
visio(n-), from *videre 'to see.'*

What

Creating vision is a life coaching skill that unlocks the client's ability to imagine an experience in the future. Both coach and client must trust the client's own imagination. Vision is such a central element to life coaching because coaches can help clients clearly see what is possible for them in the future. It encourages them to use their imagination to think of what it will be like in that future position. It is one of the best tools that coaches have. Helping clients use vision in their lives has five components:

- **Imagination.** Imagination is central to the vision process. Jumping into a vision for the future is an act of faith and requires trusting the imagination and allowing the vision to take shape.

- **Awareness of what is most important.** There are no right or wrong answers when it comes to vision and what a client wants in the future. Sometimes it is a challenge for clients to answer questions that have no right or wrong answers. Part of what makes vision so useful is that instead of looking for what is right or wrong, coaches look for what seems to have the most impact and what aligns with the client's values. Vision requires awareness of the client's priorities.

- **The bigger picture.** Vision often requires looking at something from a larger point of view and identifying the significance of the current action.

- **Little details.** Vision sometimes requires looking at the minute details of the future and making those little details more visceral.

- **Stamina.** Using imagination requires energy and stamina, especially if the client is not used to tapping into imagination in this way. Staying focused on what life will be like in the future can be a challenge. A coach's well-developed stamina and ability to stick with clients for longer periods is a vital skill.

- **Exercises that use vision.** The following three exercises focus on using vision to help your client gain a clearer understanding:

  - Future-Self

  - Bird's eye View

  - Inner Critic

Why

- **Is pragmatic.** Creating a vision is the first step in making a well-designed action or achieving any other outcome that the client seeks. Rarely does a client take the time out of his or her busy life to sit back and think specifically about what she or he wants for the future. The client can leverage her or his time by determining the best action to take, avoiding time wasted on things that will not ultimately lead to the larger vision. So, while taking time to think about a vision does not appear to move a client forward quickly, it is actually one of the most useful and pragmatic ways to clarify desires and goals.

- **Feeds hope and mitigates delayed gratification.** Creating a vision and adding details, especially to one that has a lot of meaning for the client, is a way of making the future vision more real in the face of present circumstances. That hope for the future keeps the client moving forward and helps him or her cope with delaying gratification. The client learns the value of putting work into his or her vision. Actions become vital to achieving that vision of the future. Vision is a central element to managing motivation positively and sustainably.

- **Provides a new perspective.** When using vision, paying attention to a new point of view is powerful for the client. For example, the *Bird's Eye View* perspective (see chapter 8) gives the client the opportunity to imagine all of the little details while also looking at the bigger picture.

When imagining the *Future-Self* (see session 17, the client creates the perspective looking back from fifteen years in the future.

- **Takes practice.** Imagination gets better with practice, especially when the client starts by creating a vision for just a few weeks into the future and then takes steps to make the vision happen. The experience can be surreal when he or she realizes that it is possible for the imagined vision to be achieved – to literally live his or her dream. Excitement builds as a result of understanding the visioning practice. One experience of a successfully achieved vision will help clients create additional vivid and useful pictures for other things they want in their future.

- **Highlights potential obstacles.** During the course of creating a vision, clients can identify potential obstacles and create preemptive methods to overcome these obstacles.

- **Pinpoints needed resources.** In the same way that visioning helps a client become aware of obstacles, it can also help her or him to understand what resources need to be emphasized, developed, or sought out.

- **Calls out a specific action and when it needs to happen.** Often, the client feels "vertigo" when becoming aware of all the steps necessary for something to happen. For example, a client might make the decision to get up early on Tuesday and exercise. However, that decision is not made on Tuesday morning. More likely, the decision was made Monday evening while sitting around. The process can help the client determine specifically when he or she will follow through. Vision can help the client create a system to make decisions that are based on values.

How

Future pacing is jumping to some point in the future and imagining what that reality will be like. This is an important part of the vision process. That timeframe could be two weeks, three months, or ten years.

1) With your client, introduce the idea of creating a vision and a structure, then become clear on the timeframe. It is usually easiest to start at three months and it provides a great structure to remind your client to use a well-designed action.

2) Ask your client powerful questions to elicit both the bigger picture view and the meaning behind creating this structure. You can also use the *Wheel of Life* as a starting point or look at one day in your client's life three months from now.

3) Now that you have identified some point in the future, pace the reality. Take your client through the steps at the speed it would really be happening, and have her or him imagine what that would be like.

4) Imagine and capture the little details. Once the timeframe, bigger picture, and reasons are clear, the next step is to flesh out the vision with specifics. Sometimes those details are the most valuable part and make the exercise come to life for your client.

5) Design the structure for your client to be reminded of this vision. Determine how your client wants to capture this vision. Does he or she want to create a sound recording of what a day in his or her life will be like? Does he or she want to create a series of images? How often will your client be reminded of this vision?

6) Repeat the process. Three months will pass by, and your client will have the opportunity to be in the timeframe of the vision. Once a client has the experience of living one vision, she or he can fine tune the next vision and create a new structure for the next most feasible timeframe.

Vision Recording

A client's Vision Recording is essentially a tool to focus energy and overcome limiting beliefs. It relies on your client's imagination by asking him or her to create a vivid vision of what the future could be. The exercise primes your client for future exercises in the *Academic Life Coaching Program*. The recording also captures that first vision of what your client wanted to accomplish. One day your client can look back in awe at the power of imagination and action once the goal is actually accomplished.

Students can also opt to create a written version, an illustration, or a collection of pictures without recording themselves, that serves the same purpose. You can co-create with your client whatever works best. The Vision Recording exercise can be found in the *Academic Life Coaching Workbook*.

What

- **Sound recording.** A vision recording is a sound recording, usually about three to five minutes long, that records someone's future goals and outcomes with some music in the background.

- **Specific imagery**. The more specific and detailed the vision recording, the better. Tangible realities, such as holding a job offer letter or seeing the smile on your first paying client's face, are great specific images that are useful for the recording.

- **Short and simple sentences** It's best not to get too complicated. Simple is good.

- **Present or past tense *(not future)*.** Verbs used are in the present or past tense, not the future. When researching the power of mental training and visualization (for instance what Olympians do to train), it was often mentioned how the most useful visualizations are in the present tense, imagining the event *as it's happening,* or looking back at the accomplishment *as if it has already happened*. The technical term is called *future pacing.*

- **Importance of emotion.** Along with the details and the setting, it is important to get into the emotion of the moment. What does it feel like – or what did it feel like – to have accomplished this?

Why

- **Provides motivation towards what they want.** The recording reminds clients of what's possible and helps them tap into motivation towards the future that they want.

- **Boosts the mood.** Music evokes emotion, and there is something deeply emotional about hearing yourself describe your goals set to music. It's an immediate mood booster.

- **Makes motivation habitual.** Motivation styles are habitual. Listening to one's vision recording makes changing motivation habits much easier because the mind is constantly reminded of the new scenario your client wants to create.

How

1) Introduce the concept of creating a vision recording or another structure, such as a collage or illustration, to help the client move forward consistently with a strong focus in mind.

2) Have clients do another *Wheel of Life*. However, instead of going through and rating where they are currently, ask clients to explore what would happen (what their life would look like, emotions they would experience, etc.) if each area were a perfect 10.

3) The wheel will include some goals (things that don't fit the well-designed action model). Your job is to help your client identify steps taken and habits formed in addition to the goals outlined. Ideally, your client will create a balance of both big-picture goals and well-designed actions for the recording.

4) If you have time in the session, it is helpful to write out a practice script and make notes your client can use when recording.

Metaphor

metaphor |ˈmetəˌfôr; -fər|

noun
a figure of speech in which a word or phrase is applied to an object or action to which it is not literally applicable.
• a thing regarded as representative or symbolic of something else, esp. something abstract.
ORIGIN late 15th century: from French *métaphore*, via Latin from Greek *metaphora*, from *metapherein 'to transfer.'*

What

As a life coaching skill, the use of metaphor creates an image in the client's mind that captures an important thought, making it more memorable and useful for her or him. An outstanding metaphor can help the client wrap her or his mind around something that may have been difficult. It is also a useful tool when a coach tries to explain something difficult as it helps the client take that first step towards understanding. The three elements of using a metaphor are:

- **The object or action.** An understanding of the original object or action the client is describing.

- **Imagination.** Employing imagination to create a symbol for that original object.

- **Invitation to the client to make it his or her own**. Perhaps your client can think of a better metaphor for the issue at hand.

Why

- **Can capture a thought that is difficult to express.** Metaphors are our imagination's way of using symbols to connect us to the thoughts we find most difficult to connect to.

- **Is easy to remember.** Metaphors are often easy to remember, can carry deep meaning, and have the potential to stay with a client for years.

- **Uses the imagination.** Metaphors help clients flex their imagination and think about their situation differently. When a coach asks the client to make the metaphor fit her or him specifically, the coach is also opening up the possibility for the client to further enhance the metaphor and tap into her or his creativity.

How

1) Trust yourself as coach. Confidence is half the challenge.

2) Create a metaphor using your creativity and intuition.

3) Invite your client to make it his or her own by asking if the metaphor fits. If not, ask what he or she would change to make it fit.

4) Follow up with powerful questions to ensure that you are back in Level Two listening. Pay close attention to the pace of the coaching session.

Sample Questions about Metaphor:

- What metaphor would describe the transformation that you're experiencing right now?

- In your life's journey, what animal are you being now, and what animal do you hope to become?

- If your life was a book in three chapters, and chapter one describes where you were, chapter two describes where you are now, and chapter three describes where you're going, what would the title and summaries be of each chapter?

- What metaphor could represent the challenges you're facing?

- What metaphor could represent what it will be like when you achieve your goals?

Challenge

challenge |ˈch alənj|

noun
1 a call to take part in a contest or competition.
• a task or situation that tests someone's abilities.
2 an objection or query as to the truth of something, often with an implicit demand for proof.
verb
invite (someone) to do something that one thinks will be difficult.
• test the abilities of.
ORIGIN Middle English (in the senses [accusation] and [accuse]): from Old French chalenge (noun), chalenger (verb), from Latin calumnia 'calumny,' calumniari 'calumniate.'

What

Challenge is one of my favorite coaching tools. It is closely related to the championing tool, and the two used together can be extremely effective. However, both tools are best used sparingly. If used too often, they exhaust both coach and client by creating a life coaching session that has created a massive to do list for the client yet feels flat without taking a deeper dive into the meaning or emotion behind the actions. Used mindfully, challenge is an elegant tool that busts limiting beliefs quickly and inspires clients to take bolder actions than previously considered. Elements of challenge include:

- **Bold question**. A challenge is a question that boldly assumes your client can achieve something well beyond what she or he previously considered. For example, if your client has a goal of contacting three people in the next week to work on some community leadership practice, you could ask your client what it would be like to contact twenty people.

- **Busting previous boundaries.** Challenging is a process that busts previous boundaries. Helping your client dream and imagine what it would be like to push himself or herself further than ever before is an important element in an effective challenge. By focusing on your client's ability as well as the assumptions your client is making, you can address his or her learning, which leads to valuable insights.

- **Counter offer.** The bold question pushes the boundaries of what your client thought was possible. Sometimes clients accept the challenge at face value. However, clients often balk at the suggestion and come back with a flat out "no" or counter offer. The counter offer stage provides the chance to explore assumptions, details, well-designed actions, and the nitty-gritty of what it will take to accomplish the desired outcome.

- **Continued curiosity.** Whether or not your client takes the challenge is not as important as your continued curiosity as a coach. An effective challenge can have a profound effect on your client's thinking and emotions. It is helpful to remain unattached to whether or not your client accepts your challenge, stay curious, and remain in coaching mode. Let the tool do the work for you as your client wrestles with assumptions, dreams, and committing to ambitious accountabilities.

Why

- **Discovers boundaries.** Part of what makes challenging effective is its ability to uncover boundaries about what a client thinks is possible. Clients often respond to a challenge with disbelief, but their boundaries of what they think is possible have been expanded. Most clients reject a challenge at first. (If they do not, the challenge is not big enough.) In response, most clients respond with an action smaller than the challenge, but bolder than they would have originally considered.

- **Expands the brainstorming process.** A client may not accept the coach's original challenge, but may come up with an equally grand action.

- **Underscores the coach's belief in the client.** A challenge points to the coach's belief in the client's capabilities.

- **Pushes the client out of his or her comfort zone.** In order for clients to grow, they need to take risks and try new things.

- **Plays into a client's personality strengths.** A challenge is exciting. Depending on the client's core motivation type, a challenge can be a boon to his or her excitement level.

How

1) While listening to your client describe the action she or he is going to take, think about what action could be four or five levels bigger.

2) You can ask permission or simply jump to your challenge.

3) Pay close attention to your client's reaction. Disbelief? Curiosity? Excitement? Stay in Level Two listening. Resist the temptation to go to Level One listening.

4) Follow up by asking your client if he or she wants to take a different action. If your client does not want to meet the challenge, what steps is he or she excited to take?

5) Ask powerful questions to explore any limiting beliefs or your client's assumptions about previous boundaries.

6) Help your client create well-designed actions and accountabilities.

Sample Dialogue

Coach: Seems like you've done a fantastic job following through this past week.

Client: Thanks! For the most part I've been reviewing those notes daily, and it's really helping. It's like I'm able to go deeper into what I've learned that day and it really helps when I'm looking over the notes later and studying.

Coach: What's the next step for you?

Client: I want to keep up the habit and I'm not sure what else. I know that I'm studying well, but I still feel pressured by tests.

Coach: What makes you feel the pressure?

Client: I'm still waiting the night or two before tests to study, but I don't really see any way around that. I'm pretty busy as it is...

Coach: What if you created your study notes – basically the guide that you'll use for tests – right after class? Or the first opportunity that you have a break?

Client: No way. Sure that would be awesome, but I just don't see myself having that kind of discipline.

Coach: What stops you?

Client: I'm not sure. I just know that when I'm finished with class, studying is the last thing on my mind. I really want to take a break.

Coach: What could you fit in your day?

Client: Here's what I can do. I'll keep to the 15 minutes review. That's been working. And I'll make the more detailed notes the same night as the class. You know, that's actually a little exciting.

Coach: What's exciting about it?

Client: I've been wanting to do something like this, and I've just felt so bad about myself that I can't get myself disciplined enough to ask professors about questions I have because it always seems like it's too late and the test is the next day.

Chapter 10: Systems

Questions to Consider

Systems

- Why is the word "organization" usually received so poorly by students?

- Why are systems one answer to effectively handle stress?

- Why is paying attention to the energy required to run the system important?

- How does thinking in terms of a system take away personal judgment?

Recipe for Academic Success

- What are the three ingredients for academic success?

- What is the best way to present these ingredients to students?

Systems

system |ˈsistəm|

noun
1 a set of connected things or parts forming a complex whole, in particular:
• a set of things working together as parts of a mechanism or an interconnecting network: *the state railroad system | fluid is pushed through a system of pipes or channels.*
2 a set of principles or procedures according to which something is done; an organized scheme or method: *a multiparty system of government | the public school system.*
ORIGIN early 17th cent.: from French système or late Latin systema, from Greek sustēma, from sun- 'with' + histanai 'set up.'

This is one of my favorite exercises in the *Academic Life Coaching Program*. The Systems exercise is designed to get students to be proactive, work differently, and be more effective. It can be found in the *Academic Life Coaching Workbook*. This exercise is crucially important because it helps students understand that grades are not a reflection of intelligence or innate self-worth. Rather, grades are merely a reflection of their systems and formed habits (including learning and thinking styles).

Looking at the world from a system point of view also helps students avoid procrastinating – which always prevents them from taking important action steps. The keys to using systems are:

- Students are NOT their grades. Their grades are more of a reflection of the system they are using. If they change their system, their grades are likely to improve.

- Systems are an integration of action, materials, structure, and time. The more a system is specific to *when* something takes place, *what* the material and structures are, and *what* action will take place, the stronger it will be.

- Locate the *choice points*. Systems usually spring naturally from there.

- A system will only be used if it makes the action easier and more effective than it was before. Systems need to be simple and become stronger with use, not take more time or energy.

- Effective systems often address the little details. What little thing can you add to what's already here? How can I make this more beautiful? What would make this more effective? Look for the details.

What

- **Original resources.** Everything is a resource. From the homework monster, to the plethora of papers that teachers and students create, to the amount of time you have on your hands and your level of energy, everything is considered a resource when devising a system.

- **Structures.** This is what is put in place to best use the resources. A structure can be tangible, such as a new folder system organized by what task needs to happen next. It can also be intangible or a mental habit, such as setting a reminder. A structure can also be a bit of both. For example, creating a well-designed action for a client to place his or her planner open on the desk at the beginning of class functions as both a tangible structure (the planner) and a reminder to use it.

- **Flow.** Flow is the movement through a system in response to the structures (or lack of structures) in place. For example, the banks and the rocks in the water determine the flow of a river. Similarly, the apps and tools someone uses determines the flow of work. There is always some flow present, but flow is not always designed mindfully. When a backpack becomes messy, one could point to a lack of structure to handle the flow of papers as its cause.

- **Choice point.** A choice point is the intersection of structure and flow. For example, the decision to get the planner out on the desk at the beginning of class is the key choice point in the system. If a student follows through with that choice, then the rest of the steps fall into place. Since that action is the hinge on which the system depends, it is helpful to make that step as clear, simple, and easy as possible.

- **Outcome.** The natural outcome is what happens if the system works, but a system is only going to be used if it makes things easier. Over time, systems become habitual, and the habits become a part of the structure and flow of the system. If the outcome matches what your client wants, great! If not, then go back and tinker with the structures, and see how they interact with the natural flow.

Why

- **Structures guide flow.** Systems work because structures make hard work easier by enabling a natural flow. For example, let's consider the simple, well-designed action of placing a student's planner open on the desk at the beginning of class. Once the planner is open on the desk, the natural flow is to fill it out. In a lull, a student will casually glance over the to-do list and mentally organize his or her time. If something needs to be added from earlier in the day, it's easy. If there isn't much time to get a planner out and record the homework assignment because the bell was ringing, having the planner out makes it easier for the student to jot a quick note and finish recording the assignment at the beginning of the next class. The key to making a system work is finding structures that guide flow easily and naturally.

- **Breaks down bigger tasks into smaller tasks.** Systems work because they naturally break down bigger tasks into smaller tasks. In the planner example, the bigger task of recording to-dos from a school day is broken down into smaller parts spread out over the course of the whole day. First, get the planner out and open it. Second, when the teacher gives you the assignment, write it down. Third, put away the planner and repeat during the next class. By having to put away all of your stuff, including scooping up your open planner, the open planner serves as the reminder to write down the assignment. The system does the work of reminding and making it easy to write down to-dos. It also breaks down a bigger task into tiny, bite-sized pieces.

- **Allows for experimentation without judgment.** Some of the magic of thinking in terms of a system is removing judgment from the equation. So often people attribute success or failure to a personal character trait, which puts them in a fixed mindset. The downside to a fixed mindset is the increased pressure to be immediately successful and intensely try to avoid failure. Taking success or failure personally in a fixed mindset makes adopting a playful attitude nearly impossible. Instead, thinking in terms of systems allows your client to try out new actions and put new things in place. If they don't work, it's no big deal. Try something else. Keep trying new things with the system until something clicks.

How

1) Introduce the concept to the student. When introducing systems, an easy target is asking how messy or clean your client's room is. Clothes and laundry provide a quick visual check to see how dialed-in your client's systems are. Taking a look at academics and binder organization is also a useful exercise. A popular example is the *what-why-how* approach to creating a system for idea organization.

2) Determine the outcome your client wants to achieve. These are goals, just with a fancier name and a different mindset.

3) The next step helps the student think more in terms of systems. Ask about the starting point or the resources available to your client. Many students take resources such as time and energy for granted. Ask students to write down as many activities as possible -- homework assignments, keeping a planner, getting a snack, etc. It is even helpful to write down intangible resources such as energy, motivation, and time. Writing down all of the necessary pieces helps your client account for energy levels and time. So often we assume we have unlimited time and energy when designing systems. The best systems work even when the motivation is low and time is scarce.

4) A system – and habit – is already in place, even if it's not working too well. It's much easier to build on what's working than to scrap the whole system. Sometimes a fresh start is great. This is your client's call. Outline the current system and look for the little details and things that are working.

5) Look at what is not working. The tendency when looking at a messy room, backpack, or binder is to get in there and start cleaning things up. Although your client may immediately feel better, it hasn't solved the real problem. Within a week or two (sometimes even sooner) the mess has returned. In the process of cleaning up, your client has taken away all the evidence and clues about what structure is needed to create a great system. Avoid the urge to immediately clean up and rearrange. Instead, approach the mess like a scientist looking for clues as to what's not working so that you can create a lasting structure for what will work.

6) I tend to do the next two prompts – decision points and structures – simultaneously. The point of having decision points before structures is to get students to think in terms of time. Stuff takes time to sort. Anything your client acquires will at some point demand time and attention to move and find a place. It accelerates the process if your client can understand the places where stuff is acquired (tangible things), action (what needs to be done), and time (the time they have to do it).

7) Draw out the map of the system that includes a visual representation of raw ingredients, decision points, structures, and outcomes. Most likely, it will be similar to the illustration in the workbook. This important and useful step helps students lock in the learning about systems and move forward more quickly in creating new systems.

8) Help your client create some well-designed actions to lock in systems theory with mindfully designing structures and habits to create an efficient and effective flow.

Recipe for Academic Success

recipe |ˈresəˌpē|

noun
a set of instructions for preparing a particular dish, including a list of the ingredients required: *a traditional Indonesian recipe.*
• something that is likely to lead to a particular outcome: *sky-high interest rates are **a** recipe for disaster.*
ORIGIN late Middle English: from Latin, literally *'receive!'* (first used as an instruction in medical prescriptions), imperative of *recipere .*

success |səkˈses|

noun
the accomplishment of an aim or purpose: the president had some success in restoring confidence.
• the attainment of popularity or profit: *the success of his play.*
• a person or thing that achieves desired aims or attains prosperity: *I must make a success of my business.*
ORIGIN mid 16th cent.: from Latin *successus,* from the verb *succedere 'come close after'*

Doing well academically is not a mystery. It is a science. Yet, so many students try harder to achieve better grades, or to do so with much less stress, and it does not work well over the long run. In the *Academic Life Coaching Program* students have the opportunity to redesign an approach to school work. The Recipe for Academic Success exercise fits in nicely with systems and is essentially a list of suggested, desired outcomes. It can be found in the *Academic Life Coaching Workbook.*

This short exercise aims to give students the blueprint of the science behind getting good grades. Here are the ingredients:

1) Use a planner and a binder (In the following exercises in this session, you will lead students through creating systems.)

2) Use the student's learning and thinking style when taking notes and studying. (This section assumes that the student is indeed studying.)

3) Talk to teachers.

The key to the *Recipe for Academic Success* is to do all three (use a planner, use learning and thinking styles, and talk to teachers) at the same time. Students may perform better on tests because they are using their thinking styles for notes, and they may be even better organized, but their grades won't improve if they don't also communicate what they are doing with their teachers. The recipe works because it covers all the bases, and it's simple.

What

- **Using a planner.** Using a planner means writing daily homework assignments, study activities, or other actions that need to be completed in the planner by a certain time. I have found it is most helpful to suggest that students keep a planner open on the desk at the beginning of every class.

- **Using the academic thinking styles what, why, and how.** Using what, why, and how automatically puts students into a proactive learning mode. Students are actively seeking out these aspects of each concept.

- **Making appointments to speak with teachers.** The purpose of the student requesting a teacher appointment outside of class is to ask about methods to improve learning. The purpose is not to ask how to get a better grade. When students ask teachers how they can get better grades, it can be frustrating. Instead, teachers care about the amount and effectiveness of effort that students are putting into learning. It's more appropriate and useful for students to ask teachers, "What can I do to improve the way I learn and think?"

Why

- **Shifts to a positive mindset.** The recipe works because it shifts students from being passive to being interactive learners. The proactive learner taps into a different motivation structure in the brain, releasing positive hormones that make it easier for students to sustain stamina and energy as they take on increasingly challenging concepts. Doing work under extreme stress, or cramming a lot of information into a small amount of time triggers stress-induced hormones that can lead to a negative cycle of procrastination and frustration. The combination of using a planner with the academic thinking styles avoids this negative cycle and makes it easy for students to engage in the positive cycle of being prepared and proactive.

- **People enjoy what they understand.** The academic thinking styles make it easier to understand complex concepts. When students start to understand complex concepts better, school becomes more enjoyable, so it's easier to get motivated to learn.

- **Relieves stress.** Students often report that it is more stressful to be chronically behind and feel bad about grades than it is to be on top of the work and grades. Putting in the energy to stay on top of things in the long run results in far less stress, more motivation, and more life fulfillment.

- **Asking for help is a sign of strength.** Culturally, sometimes students think that asking for help means they are weak or not smart enough to come up with their own solution. In fact, the opposite is true. Asking for help is a sign of strength. It is a sign of being secure in who we are and in recognizing when we should reach out to others for support. Getting in the habit of asking for help and feedback is one of the most powerful personal growth habits that students can adopt.

How

1) Now it's time to get down to the business of creating systems that help students improve their grades. Many students are stressed out, making poor grades, or both. The first step is to introduce the idea of a recipe – a simple path forward – that will help your client manage stress and improve grades. It builds on the previous exercises designed to help students earn better grades with less stress.

2) Ask your client which elements of the recipe are easy and which are harder to follow through on.

3) Do some coaching on integrating each of these ingredients into your client's life.

4) Go through the prompts in the *Academic Life Coaching Workbook*.

5) The final questions attempt to build on other areas of your client's life where things are going great. The principle is to find a system where things are going well and apply the same perspective and mindset to your client's academic system.

6) Create a well-designed action for your client.

Chapter 11: Motivation Styles

Questions to Consider

Motivation Styles

- What are the different types of motivation styles?

Conditional vs. Intrinsic Motivation

- What is the benefit of conditional motivation?

- What is the cost of conditional motivation?

- What is the benefit of intrinsic motivation?

- What is the challenge of tapping into intrinsic motivation?

Reactive vs. Proactive Motivation

- What are the benefits and drawbacks of being motivated away from something?

- What are the benefits of being motivated towards something?

- What are the usual challenges with motivation?

Self vs. Empathetic Motivation

- In your own life, where do you find yourself being motivated for the sake of self?

- For the sake of others?

Motivation Styles

motivation | ˌmōtəˈvāSHən|

noun
the reason or reasons one has for acting or behaving in a particular way: *escape can be a strong motivation for travel.*
• the general desire or willingness of someone to do something: *keep staff up to date and maintain interest and motivation.*
ORIGIN late 19th cent.: from motive, reinforced by motivate.

The quality of motivation matters because it sparks action and continues to push clients to take steps forward when the going gets tough. Understanding specific styles of motivation – intrinsic versus conditional, proactive (toward benefit) versus reactive (away from threat), and self-interest versus empathetic – helps your client develop a more refined ability and flexibility to employ all styles. Each style has its own benefits and drawbacks. To continually push potential, we need each style. The following exercise helps your client become aware of each style and understand why it is important to tap into the different styles at different times.

Motivation starts with having a vision that compels action. In client session number two, students finished the session by creating a compelling action from a compelling vision of what they want to achieve three to four months in the future. The three – to four – month mark is important in creating a vision because it's far enough into the future that students can get excited and dream about what is possible. The three – to four – month mark is also close enough that it leads to tangible action steps and can feel immediate and somewhat pressing.

In the previous client session, you also helped your client create a system to follow. Hopefully that system works so well that your client doesn't have to rely on willpower to create habit change. Instead, this system makes following through on the action easier than not taking action. Clients can also use the power to take actions any way that works in the short run. However, everybody has a limited stamina for willpower because it is a limited resource.

Fortunately, when clients understand distinctions in motivation styles and which motivation styles work best for them, they don't have to rely exclusively on willpower to stay on track. They can start to create systems that support and remind them of different perspectives or reasons to keep moving forward. Having an awareness of motivation styles leads to smarter, more significant action and more meaningful results.

Let's first examine the distinctions between motivation styles, the reasons why they work, and then how to use them when working with clients.

What

The *Academic Life Coaching Program* provides students with three different sets of distinctions in motivation styles and sets aside an entire session in the program to discuss them. The Motivation Styles exercise can be found in the *Academic Life Coaching Workbook*. These motivation styles address sources of motivation. They are:

- **Conditional vs. intrinsic motivation.** Intrinsic motivation is experiencing flow and joy from the activity at hand even if the activity is unpleasant. Finding intrinsic joy in unpleasant tasks is a super power that requires focus and mental discipline. It is also a habit. It becomes easier to accomplish as clients develop stronger skills to deal with drudgery and adopt a more resourceful, positive attitude. On the other hand, tapping into conditional motivation (i.e. doing something for the sake of the reward at the end of the task) is not necessarily useless. Conditional motivation can be extremely useful to get clients to move quickly. However, sustaining conditional motivation requires larger and larger payoffs, or less and less work, for the same carrot at the end of the journey.

- **Proactive vs. reactive motivation.** Proactive motivation is being motivated in advance based on a positive vision of what you are working towards. It is being motivated toward something beneficial. Reactive motivation is getting in gear because a deadline is staring you in the face, and you have to get moving now. It is being motivated away from pain. The benefit of proactive motivation is that it feels good and is easier to sustain over time. The drawback is that it's challenging to spark. Reactive motivation is easier to spark but harder to sustain over time. We need both.

- **Self vs. empathetic.** Self-motivation is being motivated for the sake of self. Empathetic motivation is being motivated for the sake of others.

Coaches looking to build a larger coaching practice experience much more anxiety and fear when they are only motivated for the sake of themselves. Tapping into motivation for the sake of others helps us get out of our own way. People are more joyful and fulfilled, and less stressed and anxious, when working for the benefit of others.

Why

- **Creates awareness.** Often individuals do not realize that there are different motivation styles. The pressure of finances, health, and family tends to drive a conditional, reactive, sake of self-motivation style. So, empowering clients with the awareness (and results) of alternative motivation styles is like providing a map to guide them out of a hazy procrastination forest. By stumbling around in the procrastination forest, clients might eventually reach the golden fields of being on top of their work, but having a map makes the journey so much faster and easier.

- **Develops stamina.** A big part of motivation and accomplishment is having the stamina to stick with frustration and setbacks long enough to experience a breakthrough. So often clients stop short in taking those next steps because stamina is low. Tapping into alternative motivation styles helps clients manage their energy differently. Like shifting into different gears in a car, leveraging alternative motivation combinations can serve different functions throughout the client's day.

- **Better mindsets lead to better results.** Perhaps the biggest reason why motivation styles work so well with clients is that experimenting with different ways to get motivated leads to a resourceful, almost playful, mindset. Any time a client is curious about trying different approaches, you have the opportunity as a coach to help your client explore different mindsets as well. The combination of different mindsets and actions is powerful and can lead to quick results, which demonstrates that the mindsets and actions are working.

Conditional vs. Intrinsic Motivation

Intrinsic motivation seems to be getting all the praise these days, and rightfully so. Tapping into intrinsic motivation – doing something hard for the sheer joy of doing it – is intertwined with the state of *flow*. Flow exists at the intersection of skill and challenge. It is that blissful experience of being immersed and fully engaged in the present moment.

Conditional motivation, on the other hand, gets the bad reputation of creating more problems than it solves. Conditional motivation is doing something only because the reward or benefit at the end of the onerous task is worth it. It is doing boring homework because you want to get an A. It is doing dull administrative work because you want to keep your job or stay in business.

The bottom line is that both intrinsic and conditional motivation are useful and necessary to lead a productive, fulfilled life.

How

When I was teaching Latin and developing the *Academic Life Coaching Program*, I found the following approaches to be the most useful to help students tap into intrinsic motivation. The full Conditional vs. Intrinsic Motivation exercise can be found in the *Academic Life Coaching Workbook*.

1) Be straightforward. Ask your client when he or she uses intrinsic or conditional motivation. It is surprising how simply raising awareness in a coaching setting, combined with curiosity, can lead to more insight and inspired action plans.

2) Use a borrowed perspective from another area of your client's life. Ask your client about an area of life where he or she easily taps into intrinsic motivation. Help your client define the perspective, recognize the pattern, and pull out details of the experience of being in flow. Then, ask your client to apply that same mindset to another area of his or her life. The client is borrowing an intrinsic perspective and applying it to another area.

3) Rely on self-realization. Developing skills and stamina can be intrinsically motivating. It feels good to work hard. Using the challenge to test personal skills and stamina puts the focus and attention on work ability rather than task execution. Such a shift can help clients tap into intrinsic motivation by making the skill development the topic, so performing the task just happens to be the playground for building the ability.

4) Try the 2% experiment. This is my personal favorite. It involves asking a client the next time he or she is in the middle of dreaded work to become curious about that 2% of joy that he or she experiences. Usually clients can find a small element of a subject that is enjoyable. If they can start to look for even little things they like about the work, it can help build more understanding. People like what they understand.

5) Finally, look for ways to make the work a game. Can I get through all this work by 2pm? Can I write in my habit tracker each day for two weeks straight? Can I keep up this streak? When clients shift their perspective to make the work a game, they invite the experience of flow, which most likely taps into intrinsic motivation.

Reactive vs. Proactive Motivation

(AKA Motivation Away From vs. Motivation Towards)

"Reactive motivation" is a fancy term for the more mundane "motivation away from." When the *Academic Life Coaching Program* was first created, I was fascinated by the difference between being motivated away from something undesired and being motivated towards something desired. The difference shows up in the quality of student work, attitudes, and success patterns. Reactive motivation invites a rollercoaster of slacking off and panicked action. When the danger or bad grade is far off, it makes sense to coast. There is no need for reaction. However, when the undesired result rears its ugly head, bam, it is time to shift into action! Students on this rollercoaster bounce between ignoring work and cramming. Professionals in this pattern bounce between procrastination and putting out fires. This motivation style can be effective in short bursts, but over time, it leads to stress overload.

Proactive motivation (or motivation towards) is beautiful, and it feels great to tap into this style. It is doing the work ahead of time and creating a system to solve problems now and in the future. The challenge is getting the gumption to do the work well before a deadline looms large. The hardest part of proactive motivation is believing that the sought after goal is achievable and can be a reality. So often, goals involve an element of chance. Even if the work is done, a student might not earn an A. You might not get that promotion or land that paying client, even if you do all the right things and put in the work. Proactive motivation works particularly well when paired with intrinsic motivation. Many of the other coaching tools in the ALC program are designed to support intrinsic and proactive motivation.

The charts and exercise clarify the difference between proactive and reactive motivation. As a coach, your job is to help clients design ways to use both forms of motivation mindfully and intentionally.

How

The Reactive vs. Proactive Motivation exercise can be found in the *Academic Life Coaching Workbook.*

1) Introduce the concepts of reactive vs. proactive motivation.

2) Give examples in your own life or in the lives of students with whom you've previously worked (with their permission, of course).

3) Use the chart illustrations to show how reactive motivation causes big dips in results. It's as if students are on a roller-coaster ride with their grades. The proactive motivation chart doesn't have the big jumps that are shown in the reactive motivation chart, but neither does it have the big dips. In the following session, you'll have the opportunity to put in place many of the tools (creating a vision/using a system) that allow students to really use the proactive motivation style. For now, it's important for your client to be aware of his or her motivation style. Continually boosting awareness is the single best method for helping students naturally change their motivation style.

4) Use the prompts in the workbook to further explore the concept of reactive vs. proactive motivation.

5) Move on to the next section, *Motivation for the Sake of Self vs. Other,* to tie these motivation styles together.

Self vs. Empathetic Motivation

(AKA Motivation for the Sake of Self vs. Other)

The *Motivation Chart* ties all the distinctions of motivation together and adds a third; motivation for the sake of self vs. other. This distinction is designed to get students thinking empathetically, in terms of the future, and the impact they want to have on the world. The aim of the exercise is for students to tap into being motivated for the sake of something larger than themselves. Being motivated for a larger cause creates a context that gives even mundane tasks a deeper meaning.

As with many of the sessions in the *Academic Life Coaching Workbook,* there is a natural progression in difficulty, both in the actual session itself and in the program. In this case, conditional motivation is related to "if-I-do-this-then-I-get-this" internal dialogue. The *Away From Pain vs. Toward Benefit* exercise takes them a little further into their motivation styles. Finally, the idea of being motivated for their own sake vs. the sake of others is the most challenging. Other sessions will address this point in greater depth.

How

The Sake of Self vs. Other Motivation exercise can be found in the *Academic Life Coaching Workbook.*

1) Introduce the concept of being motivated for the sake of yourself vs. being motivated for the sake of others or for a larger cause. I use a common example of a client who wanted to become an elementary school teacher. He had a hard time getting motivated to do well in class and pay attention to math, but when he realized that he wanted to do well for the sake of his future students, everything changed. He had a context within which to place the idea of doing well in school. It worked for him.

2) Identify the outcome your client wants. Often it is to do better in school, but it can really be any desired outcome. This exercise tends to work better if it is something that has to do with school.

3) Integrate *Motivation Away vs. Toward* and *Motivation for the Sake of Self vs. Other*. (It is a challenge to integrate the concept of intrinsic motivation because it truly is self-contained. For intrinsic motivation, the work and the reward are the same.) Go through the chart, starting in the upper left asking, "If you don't follow through with [insert the action], what will happen in your life?" Then ask, "If you do follow through, what will happen?"

4) The next two rows may require more coaching questions and examples. It's helpful to encourage your client to think about tangible results. Answers like "They will be happy" are not sufficient. Instead, it's best if your client paints a picture such as "I will see smiles on my parents' faces" or "I will see my published book at my hometown library and note that it's been checked out more than ten times." The more detailed, the better.

5) Tie the *Motivation Styles* exercise together with a few great coaching homework assignments, and make sure to closely follow up. When you are working with motivation, there are many factors that come into play. The more closely you follow up and ask parents for feedback on how your clients are doing, the better.

	Skipped it	Did it
In my life		
In the lives of others (parents or friends)		
In the future (in the lives of people you do not yet know)		

Chapter 12: Reflecting and Reminders

Questions to Consider

Reframing

- What makes reframing so useful?

Paraphrase

- What are the best uses of paraphrasing?

- What is the trap to avoid in paraphrasing too much?

Setting Reminders

- Setting reminders is also known as "dropping anchors." What does the analogy of an anchor have to do with coaching?

- What are the seven steps for setting reminders?

- Why is it effective to set reminders?

Reframing

reframe |rēˈfrām|

verb [trans.]
1 place (a picture or photograph) in a new frame.
2 frame or express (words or a concept or plan) differently.

What

- **Quick perspective shift.** Reframing is the art of expressing an event or concept from a different perspective. The coach takes what a client may consider a setback or something inconsequential and provides a different – and sometimes radical – perspective shift.

- **Client's original perspective.** Reframing is useful when your client just said something that stands out to you as a limiting belief or disempowering perspective. Being able to clearly identify the original perspective in your mind helps you flip your client's thinking when using reframing. Sometimes you can clearly define the original, limiting perspective, then reframe. Other times you can just go straight for reframing. It depends on what you think would be most useful for your client.

- **Different twist.** A quick, direct statement that includes the perspective shift is the key to effective reframing. Use many of the same words your client just said, but with a different twist that invites the client to consider a new perspective.

- **Curiosity.** By staying curious about your client's experience of considering the reframing, you ensure that you continue to partner with your client in co-creating the session. It is important to be mindful that you don't try to get your client to adopt the reframing simply because you think it would be useful.

Why

- **Provides a fresh perspective.** Reframing is an important skill in life coaching because it helps clients get to a fresh perspective quickly, which influences their attitude as well as possible actions. Because it offers a different point of view, it can almost immediately short-circuit a useless cycle of self-criticism.

- **Is elegant and efficient.** One of the reasons why reframing can be so effective is its efficiency in elegantly changing a perspective. This tool serves as a shortcut through the longer Perspectives exercise. Because it is shorter, it can be easily combined with other life coaching tools.

How

1) Start with the original idea that you think would be beneficial to reframe. It could be a limiting belief. It could be an accomplishment underplayed. It could be an accomplishment overplayed. As a coach, something usually stands out to you as a moment or statement that could be useful for your client.

2) Use a quick, direct statement that reframes what your client just said. The keys here are quick and direct.

3) Follow up with a simple question about what your client's thoughts are about the reframe.

Sample Dialogue

Client: I had a really tough conversation with my brother today. He brought up something about mom and I got so annoyed. I usually wouldn't say anything to him about what I thought. But I know that I'm working on being more... confrontational... that's not the word... what was the word that we talked about last week? Oh I remember, it was 'assertive.'

Coach: Yes, that's it!

Client: I was trying to be assertive before I got really mad, but then... boom... I'm in a tough conversation I do not want to be in.

Coach: What was the outcome of the conversation?

Client: Actually, my brother thought it was kind of cool that I said something, but that was after 20 minutes of him being mad and saying how immature I was.

Coach: Seems like a successful and assertive conversation to me – and yes, I can imagine that it was tough – but it seems that it's more accurate to call it a necessary and assertive talk.

Client: Afterwards, I was in a weird way... I don't know how to say it...

Coach: Proud?

Client: Totally. Proud. I felt proud.

Paraphrase

paraphrase |ˈparəˌfrāz|

verb
express the meaning using different words, esp. to achieve greater clarity.
noun
a rewording of something written or spoken by someone else.
ORIGIN mid 16th cent. (as a noun): via Latin from Greek *paraphrasis*, from *paraphrazein*, from *para-* (expressing modification) + *phrazein* 'tell.'

What

- **Reflection.** Paraphrase is repeating back either word-for-word or slightly changing the words your client just used for the sake of your client's reflection. Reflection allows your client to think more deeply about what he or she just said and is a natural way to go deeper.

- **Brief.** This tool is most effective when the paraphrase is brief, not a long rehashing of a story or point for the benefit of the coach's understanding. Your understanding as a coach is simply not that important. What is important is continuing to ask powerful questions that get your client to consider new ideas and break new ground. Frequent, long paraphrasing mimics counseling and gets in the way of truly partnering with your client in a coaching session. The key to effective paraphrasing is keeping it brief.

- **Pause.** An important aspect of paraphrasing is pausing afterwards to allow your client time to reflect and consider what you just said. A few words of reflection and paraphrase followed by a mindful pause can have a profound effect on a client.

Why

- **Shifts the perspective.** One of the most effective uses of paraphrase is saying the words from a slightly different point of view. By using different words, a coach shifts the perspective so that the client can see things a little differently. That difference may lead to a shift in the client's thinking and can eventually lead to great insights. Paraphrase is one method to reframe a situation.

- **Provides clarity.** Paraphrase is also effective because it gives the client a chance to clarify exactly what she or he is thinking. The client's words are the most important, and by paraphrasing, a coach offers the opportunity for the client to either take the coach's words and run with them or change them to words that the client can fully own. Paraphrase also gives the coach the opportunity to clearly understand what the client is saying.

How

1) Listen carefully to what your client is saying. Pick up on individual words but also comprehending the larger meaning.

2) With a mixture of intuition and curiosity, rephrase what your client has said, adding a slight reframe or subtle shift in the point of view.

3) Be open to your client paraphrasing your paraphrase. It's only fair. At its best, paraphrase opens a new direction of exploration for you and your client.

Sample Dialogue

Client: I had a terrible day.

Coach: I'm sorry to hear that. What happened?

Client: I have so much to do. And I wrote so much down in my planner today, which was pretty big for me because I usually just shut down, but I followed through on what we talked about last week. But I got so discouraged this morning when I got a C on my physics test and I don't feel like doing any of the homework.

Coach: So you had a setback in the morning, but you still followed through on the action you created last week. But now you're not feeling that motivated. [Here is the paraphrase. Notice how the coach picks up on follow-through yet added the word 'still.']

Client: Yeah that's it. And when I was writing things down in my planner I thought to myself, "There is no way I'm going to do this." It almost became a joke.

Coach: I think you had a fantastic day. You had a setback but still followed through on the important action and you have the rest of this evening after the session to recover and get back on the horse. [See the reframing and notice that the coach again emphasizes that the student still followed through.]

Setting Reminders

reminder |riˈmīndər|

noun

a thing that causes someone to remember something: the watchtower is a reminder of the days when an enemy might appear at any moment.
• a message or communication designed to ensure that someone remembers something.
• a letter sent to remind someone of an obligation, especially to pay a bill.

Setting reminders leverages the systems, structures philosophy, and applies it to the inner world of thought and emotion. A successful reminder is a structure to help your client recover quickly. For example, they may choose a powerful perspective or value he or she wants to remember at a critical moment. The original name, "dropping anchors," was a nod to the metaphor of a ship dropping its anchor on shore close to where it wanted to stay. With this exercise, you help your client associate an easily remembered body movement, specific word, image, color – or something else a little unusual – to a chosen perspective that your client will use at a crucial decision point. By doing so, you have helped your client create a powerful reminder that calls forth internal resources when most needed. For example, let's say your client wants to be reminded of calm confidence before taking a test. You could help your client create a quick hand movement to serve as a reminder that she or he could use while walking into an exam. You can find the Setting Reminders exercise in the *Academic Life Coaching Workbook*.

What

- **Desired mindset.** The desired mindset is the concept, empowering belief, or perspective that your client wants to be able to bring back to mind when needed.

- **The reminder.** The most useful reminders are typically simple, such as applying a little bit of pressure on your hand or a subtle hand movement.

- **Association.** Setting reminders involves asking your client to associate the desired mindset with a reminder, such as the aforementioned pressure on the hand or subtle hand movement. To help your client associate the mindset and reminder, you will lead your client through exploring past memories when the mindset was present, as well as imagining future situations when your client will use the reminder to evoke the mindset.

- **Break state.** A break state is purposely asking your client to think of something unrelated to interrupt a stream of thought. For example, you might want to ask your client about what he or she had for breakfast. The purpose of the break state is to test the strength of the reminder. It's easy to be reminded of something if you're currently feeling it. Asking your client to think of something unusual, then going back to test the reminder helps ensure that the association was successful.

- **Testing the Reminder.** Testing the reminder is asking your client to do the hand motion to determine the degree to which it brings back the desired mindset. (Most times when clients do this, they smile if the association worked.) In association, you ask your client to first think of the desired mindset, then do the hand motion. Testing and using the reminder works in the opposite direction. If it works, the hand motion will evoke the desired mindset.

Why

- **Provides clarity and value.** The first step, clarifying the specific concept of which your client wants to be reminded, provides value for your client. It helps create a focal point for the next two weeks or beyond.

- **Stimulates conscious association.** Simple Pavlovian association is a powerful force in human (and animal) nature. Most of the time, association happens unconsciously. In this exercise, we make the associative process conscious. Like all association, the process works best if it is used often and reinforced.

How

1) Identify a perspective of which your client needs to be reminded when things get hard OR a future point in time when such a perspective will be most needed.

2) Enrich that perspective by asking questions like: "If your perspective had a feeling, what would that feeling be?" "If it had a color, what color is it?" "Remember a time in your life when you've felt this perspective. What was going on?" "In this perspective, what kinds of things do you say to yourself?" Use your coaching skills to draw out the perspective and make it more vivid for your client.

3) Make up a word, image, or body movement to associate with the perspective. One favorite is applying a little pressure on the part of the hand between the thumb and index finger.

4) Invite your client to relax as you help him or her associate the chosen perspective, with all of its richness, to the specific word, image, or body movement. You can combine associations to link to the chosen perspective.

5) Ask you client to describe the perspective. Just at the peak of emotion, or when you sense your client is really in the perspective, ask her or him to make an association. For example, apply a little more pressure to the hand or think of the word or color. Whatever the reminder is, invoke it a few times while your client talks about the perspective and the desired experience.

6) Repeat the previous step a few times. Repeat the reminder as you lead your client through visualizations, associating the reminder with the perspective.

7) Test the reminder. Explain that you are going to ask your client about something completely different, then invoke the reminder to see if the reminder is linked to the perspective. (This is called a "break state.") Ask your client to think about something completely different, like his or her address or zip code.

8) Ask your client to use the reminder. See if it brings back all the other images and sensations of the chosen perspective or mindset your client

wanted to remember. If it does, good. You've successfully set a reminder! If it doesn't, repeat the process. Sometimes I'll go through the process two or three times. It's perfectly fine and normal to have to repeat the process.

9) For homework, I usually ask my clients to use their reminder once a day for the next week or two. The more they use the reminder, the stronger and more useful it becomes.

Chapter 13: Assumptions and Limiting Beliefs

Questions to Consider

Assumptions, Beliefs, and Perspectives

- What is the difference between assumptions, beliefs, and perspectives?

Assumption Chart

- What is the importance of the chart in helping clients understand the impact of their assumptions?

- Why is it important to do a negative Assumption Chart with students first?

Busting Limiting Beliefs

- What are the two most common types of limiting beliefs?

- How does listening for limiting beliefs change your coaching sessions?

Assumptions, Beliefs, and Perspectives

Our thoughts have a huge impact on our actions. The ability to change perspectives while being aware of assumptions is one of the most important skills clients can learn. Even a subtle shift in perspective can make a huge difference in results. No matter what kinds of actions a student tries to take, if the assumption is dismal and negative, the action is most likely doomed to fail.

Being proven wrong is extremely stressful. People will often go to great lengths to avoid being wrong. In addition, most students are not aware of how easy it is to shift to a different perspective, much less what a perspective is. Even fewer understand how to use assumptions and perspectives to their advantage. Client Session 4 in the *Academic Life Coaching Workbook* works to empower students with this knowledge.

The assumption chart in the *Academic Life Coaching Workbook* is a popular exercise similar to limiting beliefs and signature perspectives. By design, you'll cover all three exercises in the same session. All three aim at changing the way a student views himself or herself and the world. Students use all three of these nearly interchangeably, and your client will find the one or two exercises that work best and run with that.

Often the difference between an assumption, a belief, and a perspective can get muddy. For the sake of the exercises (as well as to keep things clear in your mind), I make the following distinctions among the three concepts.

- An **assumption** is what a student thinks about something that **hasn't ever been tested**. Assumptions are picked up from other people or deduced from past experience.

- A **belief**, especially a limiting belief, is an idea that **has been accepted as being true**.

- A **perspective** is a bundle of beliefs that includes an emotion and **acts as a lens,** affecting how information and experiences are interpreted.

The curriculum introduces these exercises in the order of assumptions, beliefs, then perspectives, as a crescendo in difficulty. This progression also works to give students an understanding of the mechanics of assumptions to beliefs, beliefs to action, and action to evidence. (It also happens to be alphabetical, like biology, chemistry, and physics, which you took in that order because it was alphabetical.)

Assumption Chart & Busting Limiting Beliefs

assumption |əˈsəm(p) sh ən|

noun
1 a thing that is accepted as true or as certain to happen, without proof.
ORIGIN Middle English (sense 3) : from Old French *asompsion* or Latin *assumptio(n-)*, from the verb *assumere* (see assume).

belief |biˈlēf|

noun
1 an acceptance that a statement is true or that something exists.
• something one accepts as true or real; a firmly held opinion or conviction.
2 (belief in) trust, faith, or confidence in someone or something.
ORIGIN Middle English: alteration of Old English *gelēafa*; compare with believe .

What

An assumption is an idea believed to be true without being tested. A belief is an idea that has been accepted as true, usually with some evidence (or at least the semblance of evidence). Making distinctions and being exact is useful in the context of life coaching sessions, but for the purposes of this section, assumptions and beliefs will be treated the same since the same procedure applies for busting both.

Assumptions and beliefs can be either useful or limiting, and life coaching is particularly effective at ferreting out a client's negative assumptions and limiting beliefs in order to replace them with assumptions and beliefs that can be used to move forward. Replacing a negative assumption or busting a limiting belief has three main parts:

- **Isolating the idea.** Identifying the essence of an idea is an important part of understanding the mechanics and system for replacing negative assumptions and busting limiting beliefs.

- **Finding the disconnect.** Perhaps, at one point, the idea would have been useful to the client, but in the current circumstances, the idea limits the client's forward movement. A limiting belief impedes the client's progress precisely because it no longer makes sense.

- **Busting the negative assumption or limiting belief.** Busting a negative assumption or limiting belief means directly addressing it and identifying new assumptions, beliefs, and actions to take the place of the outdated, negative ones.

Why

- **Human beings like to be right.** Human nature wants assumptions to be true, even if it goes against what a person really wants. Why? Because it is extremely stressful to be inaccurate in our beliefs about the world and ourselves. A client's assumptions give rise to a perspective which, when combined with action, has a strong influence on the final outcome. That outcome is usually taken as evidence to support the client's original assumption. One can say it's similar in concept to a self-fulfilling prophecy.

- **Gets to the root of the problem.** It works because it gets to the root of the problem: the assumptions that clients make about who they are as a person, an area of their life, or a task they are trying to accomplish. Assumptions quickly lead to perspectives, which influence the action taken. Those three – assumptions, perspectives, and action – determine the outcome, which becomes evidence to support the original assumption. It is why people with bad attitudes tend to have bad things happen and get bad results. Fortunately, the reverse is true for people who cultivate a positive perspective.

- **Increases awareness.** Life coaching excels at helping clients become aware of outdated assumptions and beliefs. More often than not, simply becoming aware of such assumptions and beliefs helps clients discard them. This exercise helps clients see how their negative assumptions and limiting beliefs are affecting them negatively and how they are making it harder for them to achieve what they want.

- **Promotes idea upgrade.** Busting an outdated assumption or limiting belief is like getting a software update. It can activate the newest, most efficient version of the client. Clients have the opportunity to choose those beliefs that really work and discard those that do not. It empowers clients to see that they can change to a more positive and effective way of thinking if they choose to do so.

- **Counter-examples always exist.** There are always examples, even the smallest examples or experiences, that run counter to a client's outdated assumptions and limiting beliefs. Helping clients see that holding onto outdated assumptions or limiting beliefs actually alters their perception – to the point that this mindset negates actual, contrary evidence. Identifying counter-examples is an effective way to help clients realize the power of assumptions and beliefs.

- **Nominalization.** Nominalization is the process of turning an action into an identity. It is much harder for an individual to wholly change personal characteristics or his/her self-image than to simply change behaviors. For example, a client may receive a bad grade on a test or not perform well in school for two weeks. The stack of negative grades continues to pile up, and under the circumstances, it may seem natural and perhaps useful for the client to adopt the belief, "I'm a poor student," which lowers his or her expectations in order to prevent further disappointment. However, changing an identity, like "I'm a poor student," is more challenging than changing actions. Identities tend to be deeply ingrained, while actions can be more easily designed. By changing actions, clients achieve a different outcome and thus can turn limiting beliefs into empowering beliefs.

How: The Assumption Chart

The Assumption Chart exercise can be found in the *Academic Life Coaching Workbook*.

1) Explain to your client what an assumption is and the relationship between assumptions and evidence.

   - Assumption: to take up an unproven thought and act as if it is true, or to take it for granted.

   - Process: an assumption quickly leads to a perspective, which has an impact on action taken.

- Evidence: action based on an assumption directly leads to results, which become evidence and almost always reinforce the original assumption.

2) Using an area in your client's life that may or may not be going so well, ask her or him about some of the original assumptions she or he has made about this area (i.e. an assumption of what it would be like to talk with a teacher, bring up a certain topic with parents, or try something new). (Sometimes the assumptions get mixed together with a limiting belief. It is completely OK if that happens. For the sake of these exercises, assumptions and limiting beliefs are synonymous. However, once your client understands the difference between assumptions and beliefs, it helps her or him avoid negative assumptions before they become entrenched as limiting beliefs.)

3) Isolate one assumption. It is typically something like, "Talking to teachers is difficult."

4) Explore what perspectives arise out of that assumption, and write it down in the square in the bottom left area of the chart below.

5) Next, explore what kinds of actions are most likely to be taken from that perspective. Write it down in the bottom right area.

6) Determine what kind of results will most likely occur from the action, which quickly becomes the evidence that reinforces the assumption.

7) This exercise can bring up a lot of great insights and material to use as a basis for coaching. Coach away!

8) Repeat the process using the assumption chart with a positive assumption, starting with the assumption, then going counter-clockwise through the assumption chart.

9) Have your client compare the two charts and coach on: How will your client know which chart he or she is in? What can your client do as a reminder to act from the positive assumption?

10) Any other coaching questions that compare the two states of being are great to use!

11) Create coaching homework on staying in the realm of the positive assumption chart for the next two weeks and see what happens.

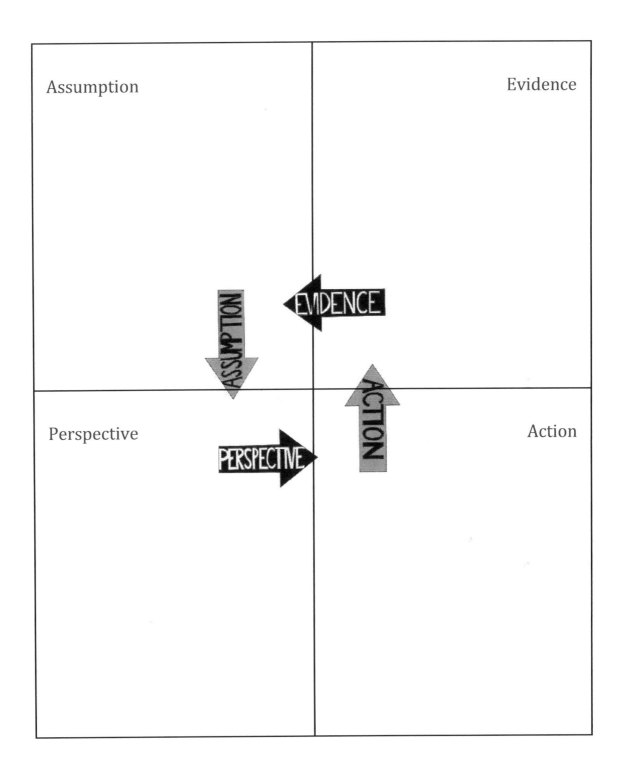

How: Busting Limiting Beliefs

The key to making the *Busting Limiting Beliefs* exercise work is to find the counter examples; those little examples that fly in the face of limiting beliefs. Even a small example can create a crack in the previous limiting belief and offer a small gap for another belief to take its place. Look for those small cracks.

It is also important to be mindful of nominalization, the process of turning an action, such as getting a poor grade on a test, into a noun, such as "poor student." The *Busting Limiting Beliefs* exercise is designed to reverse this process and help students realize the results they are getting derive from the beliefs and system they are using, NOT their innate self-worth or talent.

After the exercise brings up insights and aha moments for your client, go with it. Jump to other exercises, such as creating a system or a structure, to lock in the learning. Soon that belief becomes a perspective, and perspectives are extremely habitual.

The *Busting Limiting Beliefs* exercise can be found in the *Academic Life Coaching Workbook*.

1) Explore a few areas in your client's life that are not going well or places where he or she isn't getting the desired results. This often has to do with grades, relationships with parents or friends, getting into a particular university, or sports.

2) Pick one area to start the process.

3) Help your client with brainstorming a list of beliefs about himself or herself or about the topic. Feel free to participate fully in the brainstorming, throwing out possible ideas that your client may or may not have to help the process along. Intuition is powerful, and brainstorming often leads to great insights.

4) Circle the helpful beliefs. Cross out the limiting beliefs with a single line so they can still be read.

5) Next to the crossed-out limiting belief, write the opposite belief. It is important to have fun with this next step and to encourage your client to suspend judgment and go with the process.

6) Ask your client, "In what ways is the new, empowering belief true?" The key here is to look for the counter-examples in your client's life

when the empowering belief is true, even if it is just a small example, or even if it is true in a small way. This step is crucial to the success of the exercise, and this is where your coaching skills really come into play.

7) After you have identified several areas in which the new empowered belief could possibly be true, take it to the next level by asking your client, "What action would you take if you fully believed the new, empowering belief?" Write out the actions in the space provided.

8) Create accountability for the new, empowering belief and give your client some coaching homework to act on this new belief.

Chapter 14: Perspectives

Questions to Consider

Perspectives

- What is a default perspective?

- What makes up a perspective?

- Why do perspectives matter?

Perspectives

perspective |pərˈspektiv|

noun

a particular attitude toward or way of regarding something; a point of view.
• true understanding of the relative importance of things; a sense of proportion
ORIGIN late Middle English (in the sense 'optics'): from medieval Latin perspectiva (ars) 'science of optics,' from perspect- 'looked at closely,' from the verb perspicere, from per- 'through' + specere 'to look.'

attitude |ˈatiˌt(y)oōd|

noun

a settled way of thinking or feeling about someone or something, typically one that is reflected in a person's behavior.
• a position of the body proper to or implying an action or mental state.
• informal individuality and self-confidence as manifested by behavior or appearance.
ORIGIN late 17th cent. (denoting the placing or posture of a figure in art): from French, from Italian *attitudine* *'fitness, posture,'* from late Latin *aptitudo,* from *aptus* *'fit.'*

Most high school students have heard about the importance of having a positive attitude. Indeed, like goals and organization, having a positive attitude is a great asset, but it's overused and not particularly helpful for high school students. Clients slip in and out of a myriad of perspectives throughout the day, depending on the circumstances they encounter, but they also draw on a handful of default perspectives to make sense of themselves and the world. It is important for coach and client to identify the client's default perspectives. However, it is also important to create and shift to empowering perspectives that engage with reality in a meaningful way and lead to effective action.

By this point in the curriculum, the *Assumption Chart* and the *Busting Limiting Beliefs* exercises have helped your client shift thoughts on a few topics. Now it's time for your client to take a huge leap and begin to create a few powerful perspectives. These perspectives should be easy to access and help consistently drive positive, effective action. The *Signature Perspective* exercise gives students the tools to directly address their attitudes and get at the root cause. It can be found in the *Academic Life Coaching Workbook*. Perspective is the filter through which they are making meaning out of their experience and perception.

What

- **Beliefs and attitudes.** A perspective is a set of beliefs and attitudes through which something is perceived. It influences perception and the action taken. It has both a mental structure and a typical emotional association. From a life coaching point of view, being able to identify the usual way a client sees himself or herself, as well as the situation, is essential for increasing self-awareness and taking more effective action.

- **A filter.** A perspective also serves as a filter through which a client sees reality. It often causes her or him to ignore or exaggerate things that do not fit within her or his perspective, make generalizations based on experience, and apply these generalizations to other experiences.

- **A lens.** Whereas assumptions and beliefs usually focus only on one part of a client's life, a perspective extends to and affects all areas of life. A perspective is a bundle of beliefs that acts as a lens to interpret information, prompt assumptions and beliefs, and drive decisions to take action. Perspectives are incredibly powerful, and much of their power comes from how quickly they become habitual.

- **A default perspective.** A default perspective is a client's "go to" perspective on life, particularly when faced with a challenge, new ideas, something out of his or her comfort zone, or resistance.

- **A signature perspective.** This is the perspective that will serve us well in order to achieve our goals. We want this perspective to be our "signature" so that our thoughts can positively influence our actions and outcomes.

Why

- **Having a certain perspective is a large part of the human experience.** Perspectives are incredibly useful to clients because they affect a client's perception of reality. It is impossible for people to see reality objectively without the filter of perspectives.

- **Since perspective shapes how a client perceives reality, its influence is undeniable.** If the client has the perspective that he or she is a bad student and then adopts a negative attitude, it is much harder to get the desired grades. On the other hand, if that same client is able to shift perspective to realize that he or she has the tools to be a good student and can adopt an eager, positive attitude, the client is able to take effective action and get better results.

- **Coach-client relationship creates perspective awareness.** The coach-client relationship is an outstanding tool for helping clients become aware of their default perspectives as well as help them to adopt useful perspectives.

How

1) Briefly explain what a perspective is and how to use perspectives in your life. It's helpful if you can share some of the perspectives that have served you well with your clients. Stories are powerful. Sometimes I even use stories from other clients (after I have received their permission to share.)

2) Start with a particular focus and identify one topic. As with the *Assumption Chart* to bust limiting beliefs, this exercise begins with a particular topic. The topic can be something that's currently challenging for your client or something that's easy. I have found it works well to refer back to the *Wheel of Life* and ask your client to pick a wedge for the topic.

3) Generate different perspectives. The *Academic Life Coaching Workbook* has space for four different perspectives. Sometimes it is a challenge for high school students to think of different perspectives. You may have to offer a few to get the ball rolling.

4) As you generate different perspectives, take a little time and explore them. Is there a default perspective that comes up? Is the default perspective useful for the client to achieve his or her goals? How would your client approach the topic differently from this perspective? Try out a different topic to see how it applies and the effect the perspective has on each topic.

5) One or two perspectives will jump off the page and be the obvious choice. If two are outstanding, combine them. This will become your client's most empowering: a signature perspective.

6) Explore what action is possible from this signature perspective. Enjoy the energy of the exercise. It is high energy and positive; clients will come out of this session glowing.

7) Create an unusual name for the signature perspective to make it easier for your client to remember. It is also helpful to design a system and structure for your client to use the new, signature perspective.

8) Design accountabilities between now and the next session.

Sample Dialogue

Coach: How are things going?

Client: Great. But with one exception. I didn't do well my first semester. Basically got 2.6. [The client here's talking about his GPA: a grade point average on a 4.0 scale]

Coach: You seem really disappointed. What are you most disappointed about?

Client: I'm frustrated because it seems like my classmates don't have to work that hard. They don't really put in that much more effort than I do and yet they get A's and B's and I have to struggle just to get a B. I mean, I know I'm not a good student, I know I am a bad student, but I really did try hard that first semester to get above a 3.0.

Coach: It seems like you're struggling against yourself and the perception that you're not a good student.

Client: When I go into class, I just don't want to be there. I wonder a lot, "What's the point?"

Coach: Is "What's the point?" the perspective you have about school?

Client: [Chuckling] Yeah, that's funny. That's exactly what I think of school.

Coach: If we were to separate the negative feeling from this perspective, what would be neutral or what would the object of this perspective be?

Client: I don't know what you mean.

Coach: It feels like your perspective of being a bad student is really influencing the way that you see school and how you behave. If we were to have a really bland description of reality that didn't include a negative perspective, what would that bland description be?

Client: Just the school. It would be just "being in school."

Coach: Great, let's go with "being in school."

Client: School works.

Coach: Seems like the perspective of being a bad student is pretty rough and not working. Do you want to find a different perspective?

Client: Sure.

Coach: What's a different perspective you could take on "being in school?"

Client: I like being with my friends.

Coach: Great. What's the "friend" perspective of being in school?

Client: That part is fine. I really enjoy it.

Coach: What part of you likes and appreciates learning?

Client: What do you mean?

Coach: I know that there is a part of you that likes to be in school and likes learning.

Client: Yeah. I almost forget about that part. I get so concerned about grades. It's so hard for me to stay motivated when I think about getting a grade on an assignment.

Coach: What perspective would you take if school was purely about learning?

Client: I would love to go to school and just think all I had to do was learn the material. I don't think I would mind doing homework. I like knowing stuff, especially stuff that I care about. The problem is, I see a lot of what we learn in school just isn't useful for getting good grades and helping me achieve my goal of going to a good college.

Coach: So the perspective is that you're doing this for the sake of a future?

Client: Yeah, sometimes I think about the future but I often get scared and feel upset.

Coach: It seems like whatever you think about your past performance affects how you see your future and creates a lot of stress.

Client: Totally.

Coach: What would be a perspective that keeps you focused on the present moment and what's in front of you without the stress of the past or future?

Client: I know all I need to do is just learn it. If I learn it, I'm fine.

Coach: The "Just learn it" perspective?

Client: That works.

Coach: What's that perspective like?

Client: It's like the only thing I need to really focus on is just what's right there in front of me. I can just let everything else fall away and just focus on that assignment. Wow, I really like thinking about it this way.

Coach: Seems like there's a lot of focus here in this perspective.

Client: Yeah. In an odd way, I feel really calm.

Coach: What action naturally comes out of the "Just learn it" perspective?

Client: Well, first I need to make sure that I take better notes in class. I didn't take good notes during classes last semester and studying for finals was so hard.

The coach and client continue their session creating well-designed actions around taking notes, studying, and finishing homework assignments from the "Just learn it" perspective.

Chapter 15: Values

Questions to Consider

Clarifying Values

- What are the differences between a value and a moral?

- What is the difference between an object value and a process value?

- Why is making the distinction between the kinds of values important?

- What does identifying a process value give your client?

Making Decisions

- What does making decisions have to do with values?

- Why is this an important concept in a life coaching session?

Clarifying Values

value |ˈvalyoō|

noun
1 the regard that something is held to deserve; the importance or preciousness of something.
• the usefulness of something considered in respect of a particular purpose.
• the relative rank, importance, or power.
2 (values) a person's principles or standards of behavior; one's judgment of what is important in life.
ORIGIN Middle English : from Old French, feminine past participle of *valoir 'be worth,'* from Latin *valere.*

Value comes from the Latin word *valere* meaning to be strong or fare well. Values are the things in our lives that we feel have the most worth and which fortify us.

In the previous chapter, your client has shaken up his or her assumptions, beliefs, and perspectives. Now it is time to explore *what's really important to your client and how he or she can live a more meaningful life.*

In the *Trademarked Values* exercise, you have the opportunity to explore, define, and clarify your client's top five values. This exercise can be found in the *Academic Life Coaching Workbook.* The idea behind a "trademarked" value is similar to the *Signature Perspective;* both exercises ask clients to identify their unique, empowering points-of-view and beliefs.

What

Values are unique to each individual and call out what is most important. A person can share values with other people, but a complete list of values is like a fingerprint. By contrast, morals are customs and beliefs about what is right and wrong, usually held by society as a whole. Ethics involve conformity with a code of conduct usually narrowed by a particular field or profession. Each society has its own moral code, and each profession has its ethical guidelines.

For life coaching purposes, values have the following main components:

• **Worth.** A value is something that the client holds to be important and have worth. If something is worth it, people are willing to give or relinquish something for the sake of it. For example, if exercise is a top value for a client, he or she is willing to give up an extra hour of sleep in the morning. If spending time with family is a value, people are willing to spend less time with friends. Values inherently imply a sense of worth and sacrifice.

- **Topic vs. process value.** From a life coaching perspective, the two kinds of values are topic (the general subject of the value) and process (a quality of the actual experience). "Family" would be a topic value. Identifying "family" as a value is a good start, but it would not qualify as a process value. "Spending time together as a family" gets closer to a process value. "That moment when family is together and everyone smiles and laughs at the same time" is a good example of a process value. The more specific and clear you can be as a coach on both topic and process values, the more useful and powerful your sessions will be in your client's life.

- **A name.** Values with names having too many words are cumbersome and not as useful as values with short, unique names. Using the example above, the "moment when everyone laughs at the same time" could be termed "shared laughter." Creating a unique name gives a value more meaning and versatility for the client. For example, the client with the value "laughter shared" may also find ways to apply it at school with friends or at work with colleagues.

- **Inspires action.** Once a value is clear and has a name, the last criterion is that a value inspires and informs action in the client's life.

Why

- **Serves as a guide for making decisions and well-designed actions.** Values are an effective guide to creating well-designed actions. Indeed, values act like a compass and a map directing a client toward the path forward. Values also form the foundation for creating a compelling vision.

- **Provides the basis of fulfillment.** Having clearly defined values – and taking action to honor those values – is the foundation for a fulfilled life. Living a life aligned with values does not always mean that a client's life will be easy, but it does mean that your client will understand the importance of aligning actions with values. Even when action is difficult to take, if it is in alignment with a client's top values, the client is avoiding inner conflict.

- **Drives a sense of purpose.** Having a defined list of the client's top values, as well as putting the list in an order, gives life a structured sense of purpose. Of course, values can and do change. However, having a clear list gives a clear sense of completeness and purpose that can simplify and enrich life.

How

1) Introduce the idea of values and the importance of finding a set of values that is unique to your client. Explain that taking action based on values is a way to achieve a more fulfilled and meaningful life. This work adds further structure and gives your client another tool for making decisions wisely.

2) Explore different areas of your client's life in an effort to determine what is most important. I often ask questions like:

- When you were at your best, what were you doing?

- Think back to a peak experience. What did you do to make it happen?

- What do you really *dislike*? (In others or in a particular task? The opposite can elicit a value.)

- If someone really knew you, what would they know about you?

- What is the *most* important thing to you? What specifically is important about it?

- If you could only take one thing with you on a trip, what would you take? Why?

- Who is a person you admire? What do you admire about that person?

- What gives you strength?

3) Help your client brainstorm fun names for her or his values. If your client can name a value – and the name is a little weird – she or he has a much better chance of remembering that value and using it to inform thinking.

4) Go into a further description of each value. This is where your coaching skills become crucial. The more detailed and meaningful the value, the more powerful it will be.

5) Once you have a list, order the list in terms of what is most important to your client. Ordering can be a challenge, but it can really test the importance of each value.

6) If a concrete accountability comes out of the coaching, great. If not, that is OK. The other exercises in the session lend themselves more to creating great coaching homework.

Making Decisions

decision |diˈsiZHən|

noun
a conclusion or resolution reached after consideration: I'll make the decision on my own | the editor's decision is final.
• the action or process of deciding something or of resolving a question: *the information was used as the basis for decision.*
• a formal judgment: last year's Supreme Court decision.
• the ability or tendency to make decisions quickly; decisiveness: *she was a woman of decision.*
ORIGIN late Middle English: from Latin *decisio(n-)*, from *decidere 'determine'*

One of the main benefits of knowing one's values is applying that knowledge to make wise decisions in alignment with values. This exercise aims to help students apply their values to the decision making process. Using the previous exercise of *Systems*, pinpoint the **actual time when your client is going to make a decision to follow through on a value or ignore the value and make a different choice**. Then, guide your client in using these newly minted values as structural support. Assist him or her in bringing more of what he or she really wants into their life. The *Making Decisions* exercise can be found in the *Academic Life Coaching Workbook*.

What

- **Clarified value.** Start with the value that you created and clarified in the previous exercise.

- **Decision point.** This is the point before your client actually takes action in alignment with the value. For example, if the action is to work out in the mornings, the actual decision point is probably the night before when your client decides to set the clothes by the bedroom door.

Why

- **Combats over-optimism.** Many well-intended actions and values are torpedoed by over-optimism. Unrealistic thinking that says, "I can just wing it or get ready from scratch in the morning" usually leads to either frustration or hustling around trying frantically to beat the clock (or sometimes a bit of both). Preparation is the key to being successful. By taking the extra step of identifying not just the value, but the action to take, and the preparation required ahead of time, your client has more tools to follow through.

- **Promotes systems thinking.** The idea of identifying the preparation and the decision point ahead of time helps you and your client think in terms of systems. Developing systems is such a powerful tool, and when you tie systems with values, you help your client develop a positive, synergistic cycle.

How

1) Transition from identifying values to identifying *when your client is going to use them to make decisions*. Describe the process and look back to a system that you jointly designed to help your client achieve something in her or his life.

2) Write down the area of focus.

3) Write a quick description of the system.

4) Identify the value most applicable to this area of focus.

5) Look at the specific point in time when your client will make a decision to honor the value, follow through, or make a different choice. Make that decision point obvious.

6) Create a new structure or modify one that already exists to help your client employ the value to make the choice.

7) Usually the exercise brings up some other insights along the way. There's a prompt to record them at the bottom. You can also apply this exercise to other areas and look for patterns in your client's life. Chances are, if she or he is doing this in one area of life, it is happening in other areas. This exercise creates a rich coaching environment to do some great work.

Values

1.

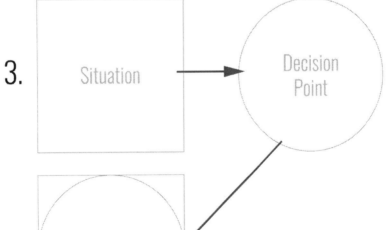

2.

3.

4.

Examples of Decision Points

- **Self-Care Value:** The point in the morning when I have to choose between hitting the snooze button or getting up for a morning jog. If I honor the Self-Care Value, I will get up and go for the jog knowing that I am taking care of myself and setting myself up for a great day. If I ignore it, I may have a few more moments of sleep, but I will feel guilty for the rest of the day, and may be a bit sluggish.

- **No Regrets Value:** The point when I decide whether to commit to hiring a web designer for my business web site or not. The web designer is waiting for my reply and before I answer him, I can either honor my No Regrets Value, or ignore it. Honoring it is asking myself if I will regret not investing in an awesome web site to promote the business of my dreams on my deathbed. Ignoring it would be to save the money, play it safe, and work on the web site myself, knowing that it would probably never be as good without professional help.

- **A-ha Moment Value:** The point at work when I have an opportunity to talk to my boss to let him know that I would like more responsibilities and that I have an interest in leadership in the workplace. I have a choice to either honor my A-ha Moment Value, which is going after opportunities where I know I can learn new things, or ignore my value and succumb to the fear of rejection or judgment from my boss.

Chapter 16: Designing the Future

Questions to Consider

Future Pacing

- What is future pacing? What are the parts?

- Why is future pacing effective?

- What is the first step in helping your client "pace" the future?

- After your client has imagined herself or himself in the future and has seen it as a movie, what can you imagine are possible next steps?

- How can you incorporate this concept into your coaching?

Self-Alignment, AKA Getting Over Jet lag

- What is the concept of jet lag?

- What is the concept of self-alignment?

- Why are these concepts effective?

- Why introduce these concepts at the halfway point in the *Academic Life Coaching Program* for students?

- What are the steps in helping clients align values to all areas of life?

Future Pacing

future |ˈfyoō ch ər|

noun
1 (usu. the future) the time or a period of time following the moment of speaking or writing; time regarded as still to come.
• events that will or are likely to happen in the time to come.
• a prospect of success or happiness.
ORIGIN late Middle English : via Old French from Latin *futurus*, future participle of *esse* *'be'* (from the stem *fu-*, ultimately from a base meaning *'grow, become'*).

This exercise is more a continuation of the *Making Decisions* exercise than one that stands on its own. It can be found in the *Academic Life Coaching Workbook* after *Making Decisions*. The idea behind *Future Pacing* is to create a vision of the future when your client makes that new and different choice. Hanging out with the daydream and adding more detail to make it real have the potential to evoke more emotion. Simply completing an intellectual exercise of integrating a value into a system may not evoke emotion. Imagining into this space significantly boosts the chances that your client will follow through with action.

Your job as a coach is to guide your client in visualizing what life will be like when he or she honors values and follows through with action. The key is to help your client imagine what life will be like once he or she has made a choice and has achieved a desired outcome.

What

- **Visualizing a specific action.** From the values exercise, your client will have a specific action in mind that he or she will want to take. Future Pacing requires that your client visualize what it will be like to follow through on that action based on a newly clarified value.

- **Next day to two-week timeline.** One of the major differences between Future Pacing and Future Self is the timeline associated with each exercise. Future Pacing usually focuses on an action coming up quickly, either the next day or in the next week or two. Future Self is a visualization exercise that is focused on jumping forward to the next decade.

Why

- **Primes follow-through.** When the time comes for your client to make the decision to take the action or pass, Future Pacing makes following through on an action more likely because it primes your client to follow through on agreed action steps.

- **Practices visualization.** From Olympic athletes in the 1980s to positive psychologists in the 2000s, visualization has proven helpful with tapping into internal resources to accomplish desired outcomes.

How

1) Use the previous exercise in *Making Decisions* to pinpoint an agreed upon time when your client will choose to follow through on a well-designed action based on values.

2) Guide your client to imagine that future point in time.

3) Ask your client, "What is it like to have made that choice?"

4) Explore the actual process of making that decision. Ask questions like "What's easy about the choice?" "What's hard about making that choice?" and "What's exciting about trying something different?"

5) Go slowly through the vision and help your client step into the reality of what making that decision will feel like. "What does it feel like the moment before you strap on your running shoes?" "What do you notice the moment after you accomplish your action?"

6) Ask what structures or additional systems your client needs to support the well-designed actions and values.

Self-Alignment, AKA Getting Over Jet Lag

jet lag |ˈdʒɛt ˌlæg|

noun
extreme tiredness and other physical effects felt by a person after a long flight across several time zones.
DERIVATIVES
jet-lagged adjective

You are now approaching the halfway mark in the *Academic Life Coaching Program,* and it is time to look at the *Wheel of Life* again with these newer tools. Self-alignment is simply using the insights gained over past sessions and closing the gap between your client's recent personal growth and old habits and beliefs that no longer fit. Self-alignment uses values as a tool to explore each aspect of your client's life with questions such as "How would you apply this new value to this area of life as well?" This is a powerful question that shortens the time it takes an insight to percolate through all areas of your client's life.

Jet lag happens when a client has an insight that moves her or him further along the path of personal growth quicker than if they would have received this insight at a later time or not at all. It's similar to what happens when you fly over a handful (or more) of time zones. The actual (local) time has accelerated, and it takes a few days for your biological clock to catch up. Recognizing such a phenomenon in a life coaching program helps cut down the time it takes your client to catch up with insights. The *Self Alignment: Getting Over Jetlag* exercise can be found in the *Academic Life Coaching Workbook.*

What

- **Original insight.** This is most likely the process value that you just created in the Values exercise (Chapter 15). However, if there is another insight your client wants to use for the exercise, that would work too.

- **Wheel of life.** In addressing the other areas or topics in your client's life, he or she has the opportunity to create a visual representation of the impact an insight can have.

- **New insights and action steps.** The exercise leads to new insights for your client and an opportunity for you to design new action steps in other areas based on the tool.

Why

- **Updates old values.** In a program designed for personal growth, newly identified values will often clash with outdated values. For example, when studying for a test, a student has a newly found intrinsic joy in learning new subjects, which clashes with an outdated value of avoiding studying. Your client now sees herself or himself as a good student, which clashes with the old value of escaping into a video game. The metaphor of jet lag helps clients see how, at one point, the old value was useful (for example, as a way to temporarily relieve stress), but less useful than the new value (in this example, which would relieve stress over time).

- **Take advantage of growth.** Like the metaphor of jet lag suggests, your client has grown in some area. Part of the journey of becoming an expert coach is being able to apply an insight from one area in a client's life to other areas. This exercise walks your client through that experience.

How

1) Briefly explain the metaphor of jet lag and how it's a natural part of the life coaching process.

2) Invite your client to do another *Wheel of Life*. This time, however, instead of looking at each area and assessing current levels of satisfaction, invite your client to apply the newly created value or signature perspective to other areas in the wheel. Ask the question, "What would be different about your approach to [name the area] if you applied [fill in the trademark value or signature perspective]?"

3) Explore what would be different.

4) This exercise creates some great coaching homework! Be sure to follow up in future sessions and return to this exercise as needed. Personal growth is a circular, not linear, process.

Chapter 17: Future Self

Questions to Consider

Future Self

- What is a future self?

- Why is the future self effective?

- What is the first step in helping your client find his or her future self?

- After your client does the future self exercise, what are the next steps?

Future Self

future |ˈfyoō ch ər|

noun
1 (usu. the future) the time or a period of time following the moment of speaking or writing; time regarded as still to come.
• events that will or are likely to happen in the time to come.
• a prospect of success or happiness.
ORIGIN late Middle English : via Old French from Latin *futurus*, future participle of *esse* *'be'* (from the stem *fu-*, ultimately from a base meaning *'grow, become'*).

self |self|

noun (pl. **selves** |selvz|)
a person's essential being that distinguishes them from others, especially considered as the object of introspection or reflexive action: *our alienation from our true selves* | [in sing.] *: guilt can be turned against the self* | *language is an aspect of a person's sense of self.*
• [with adj.] a person's particular nature or personality; the qualities that make a person individual or unique: *by the end of the round he was **back to his old self*** | *Paula seemed to be her usual cheerful self.*
• one's own interests or pleasure: *to love in an unpossessive way implies the total surrender of self.*

Studies in positive psychology have found that the vast majority of concepts we create about ourselves in the future are extremely optimistic. That optimistic future image is crucial to long-term health. Even during tough times, the future self is usually overwhelmingly positive. If your client is having a hard time creating a positive vision of life in the future, gently guide him or her to create a neutral image while gradually making the details increasingly positive. Our brains are wired to create positive future self-concepts. It is simply a matter of giving ourselves permission to tap into that wiring and follow the imagination.

The key benefit of creating a positive future self is that students can get a sense of *who they are going to be* rather than *what they are going to do.* When people ask, "What do you want to be when you grow up?" they usually mean, "What job or profession are you going to have when you grow up?" In both scenarios, it has the individual thinking only about *actions* she or he is going to take in the future without thinking about the *being.* The future self-concept can include a job or profession, but it goes beyond that by helping students get a feeling for the whole person they are growing up to be. The future self includes all the positive perspectives, experiences, and knowledge that they have gained throughout the years. Helping students tap into that inner knowing and perspective is incredibly powerful. The Future Self exercise can be found in the *Academic Life Coaching Workbook*.

What

The future self is a designed, positive perspective. It is set from the client's point of view, ten or fifteen years in the future. It is part of a series of exercises that rely heavily on using the client's imagination to create an image of himself or herself in the future. The future-self exercise has **five** different components:

- **Image of who they are going to be.** When most students think of the future, usually a specific job is the first thing that comes to mind – especially for teens. The next things tend to be family, a house, a car, and friends. The future self is an exercise that helps clients focus more on character qualities than on career or possessions. Of course, career and possessions are important, but for this exercise, we want to focus on deeper aspects of a client's life than are normally addressed.

- **Description.** Creating a detailed description of a future self adds so much value for your client. A future self has specific clothing, a geographic location, a physical description, top values, perspectives, a typical day, essentially all the things that real people have. Your client's job is to create this description using her or his imagination. Such a description helps make the positive perspective more vivid and useful.

- **Nickname.** Creating a nickname, a name that only coach and client will use to refer to the future self is often the key to helping distinguish the current perspective from that of a future self.

- **Positive perspective.** A future self includes a positive perspective that offers wisdom to your client.

- **Relationship between present and future self.** The future self represents a relationship between the client's current, default perspective and a different perspective years into the future looking back. The gap between those perspectives is personified in the relationship between the present day and future self.

Why

- **Addresses doing and being.** Most clients have dreamed of what the future holds, but the future-self exercise takes that to another level by looking at who your client will be. By imagining specific characteristics and wisdom gained through the years, your client has a method for directly addressing desired personal growth. You give your client a way to balance dreaming of both the doing (career) and the being (personal characteristics).

- **Paints an optimistic future.** Human beings naturally have an optimistic view of the distant future. The future-self is effective because it gives shape to that natural instinct and makes the future come to life.

- **Takes a strong, positive perspective.** Asking the future-self questions is equivalent to taking a strong, positive perspective. It is similar to a bird's eye view, but instead of looking at life from above, it looks at life from a time in the distant future.

How

1) Explain the concept of the future self and provide examples of your own future self and perhaps those of other clients (with your previous clients' permission).

2) Take a moment to center yourself. Take a deep breath. Shake off any remaining thoughts of a previous exercise. Encourage your client to use his or imagination and to have fun with it. Invite your client to center herself or himself, take a deep breath, and even close her or his eyes for a few seconds.

3) Ask your client to imagine a future version of herself or himself fifteen years in the future. You can lead your client through a longer future self-visualization or ask her or him to simply imagine the future-self walking into the cafe and having a seat with you. It's helpful to ask questions about:

   - Fashion style
   - Geographic location

- Description of home

- Occupation

- Typical day

- Favorite things to do

- Top values

- Message to him or her self

- Other notes

- Ask your client to create a nickname for her or his future self.

4) When you get to the "Message to you" prompt in the workbook, you are looking to help your client gain value and take action based on the image of the future self. The question can bring up many emotions. Often, future selves are very kind and often say things like, "Keep working hard." Sometimes they say, "Get your butt moving!" Whatever the message, it is a great time to use your coaching skills to bring your client to a deeper awareness of how she or he can take that message and turn it into present actions.

5) Complete the session with some coaching homework and continue to check in with the future self throughout the next few weeks

Sample Questions

Here are some examples of powerful questions about the future self. (Ideally, replace the words "future self" with the nickname that your client creates.)

- What has your future-self learned that you have yet to learn?

- When you encounter resistance, what advice does your future-self have for you?

- What is the biggest challenge that your future-self encountered between who you are now and who you'll be then? How did he or she overcome the challenge?

- What does your future-self want your present self to know?

- What does your present-self want your future self to know?

- What hopes and dreams does your future-self have for you?

- What is the biggest change that you need to make in yourself in order to complete the transformation into your future-self?

- What can you do today that your future-self will thank you for?

- What is the most powerful perspective that your future self wants you to have?

Chapter 18: Inner Critic

Questions to Consider

Inner Critic

- What is an Inner Critic?

- Why is identifying the characteristics of the Inner Critic effective?

- Why is it important to keep the Inner Critic images cartoonish?

- After your client creates an Inner Critic, what are the next steps?

Inner Critic

inner |ˈinər|

adjective [attrib.]
1 situated inside or further in; internal.
• close to the center.
2 mental or spiritual.
• (of thoughts or feelings) private and not expressed or discernible.
ORIGIN Old English *innerra*, *innra*, comparative of in .

critic |ˈkritik|

noun
1 a person who expresses an unfavorable opinion of something.
2 a person who judges the merits of literary, artistic, or musical works, esp. one who does so professionally.
ORIGIN late 16th cent.: from Latin *criticus*, from Greek *kritikos*, from *kritēs* '*a judge*,' from *krinein 'judge, decide.'*

What

We all get down on ourselves and engage in negative self-talk. The *Inner Critic* exercise is a tool used to personify negative habits, negative self-talk, and negative perspectives in order to take on a new set of more useful habits. It can be found in the *Academic Life Coaching Workbook*, before the *Future Self* exercise. The exercise is similar to debugging a software program. It takes old, outdated patterns of thought and habit, exposes them, and playfully puts them aside so that the new software can run smoothly.

At the end of the *Inner Critic* process, you will create new ground rules for your client to interact with his or her Inner Critic. It is the software update and is effective in helping your client move forward. Just the act of creating a new relationship with the Inner Critic gives your client power, and she or he will have a plan to deal with negative self-talk when it shows up again.

It is most helpful to do the *Inner Critic* exercise before the *Future Self* exercise, but the two work well in the same session. The *Inner Critic* clears the negative self-talk out of the path, and the *Future Self* fills the gaps with a stellar, positive mental structure. The *Inner Critic* exercise has three components:

- **Negative self-talk described.** Being able to describe the situation as well as the content of the negative self-talk is the foundation for this exercise.

- **Image of the Inner Critic.** It takes imagination on the part of the client to personify the negative self-talk into some sort of character (usually a cartoon character or something that corresponds to the self-talk).

- **Managing focus.** Once the Inner Critic is personified, the next step is managing focus by building a habit of setting aside the Inner Critic in favor of something else.

Why

- **Creates distance between the negative self-talk and the client's inner dialogue.** The main reason the *Inner Critic* exercise works so well is that students begin to recognize that the Inner Critic is not them. It is a vestige of a message that is no longer needed or useful. Once that message is isolated, the exercise creates distance between the client and his or her self-talk. This mental exercise increases the probability that the client will be able to dismiss that negative self-talk and focus on something more positive. Being able to separate the inner critic from who the client is and what he or she wants is very powerful.

- **Creates realization of how easy it is to dismiss negative self-talk.** Once clients have created that gap, it's easier to recognize that negative self-talk can be dismissed. Often, clients discover that they have to recover and dismiss the Inner Critic numerous times. The habit of recovery is an important part of the process and helps clients understand that they are not their Inner Critic and that they do have power over it. It is empowering for clients to learn that they have the choice to either listen to their inner critic or focus on something more useful, like their future self.

- **Is silly.** The exercise is a little silly and outside of what most clients have experienced. This silliness is one of the strengths of the exercise. Turning negative self-talk into a personified character brings an element of playfulness to the process. Such playfulness is useful in helping a client address issues that may be heavy or difficult.

How

1) Take a little time setting up the atmosphere of the coaching session. Scope out the room, especially if you are in a coffee shop, to make sure that you are in a place that allows the coaching session to go relatively uninterrupted.

2) Take an extra minute to establish a great connection with your client. Invite your clients to stretch their imagination with this exercise. Invite them to have fun and remind them to let go of judgment of themselves and of the exercise itself.

3) Explain the concept of the Inner Critic. It can be helpful to use the analogy of a software update. Explain how it is the personification of negative patterns so that your client can learn new habits.

4) Give a few examples of your own Inner Critic or the Inner Critic of students with whom you have worked. (Make sure you get their permission to share first, and do not reveal their name or other identifying characteristics.)

5) Ask your client about an area where things are not going so well or a time during the day when she or he usually has a hard time. Ask specifically, "What kinds of things do you say to yourself when you're frustrated?" or "What kinds of things do you picture?"

6) Explore the negative self-talk and perspectives. In your notes, write down the specific words your client is using.

7) Repeat the specific words used, and ask, "What do you think about a person who [fill in the negative pattern your client used]?" Keep following the thread down into the negative stuff until you feel you have reached the kernel of the negative pattern. You have found the bug, and now it is time to debug the system.

8) Ask your client, "If a little creature or being was to express that message to you, what would the creature look like?" I often use the word "little" here on purpose to keep the Inner Critic tame.

Sometimes, however, it is not little. Use your intuition and coaching skill to shift the internal message (that may be very close to your client's negative self-concept) to a personified character that can be easily overcome. Take your time. This step is the crux of the Inner Critic work!

9) Once you have the beginnings of the Inner Critic sketched out, turn to the workbook and prompt your client to answer each of the questions.

10) Keep these Inner Critics tame. In other coaching courses, the Inner Critic can be scary, huge, intimidating, mean, and ugly. However, when working with teenagers, it's especially important to avoid scary Inner Critics. Tame Inner Critics still get the job done and avoid the danger of creating an intense negative mental construct. Cartoon characters, small creatures, or funny-dressed people work well for Inner Critics.

11) After you have filled out the description, ask your client to put the Inner Critic on the other side of the table or perhaps on the other side of the room. You may need to encourage your client to use her or his imagination and have fun with the process. Put the Inner Critic underground or in a cave.

12) Facilitate a discussion between your client and the Inner Critic, exploring and creating a new way for your client to relate to the Inner Critic. Some guidelines that lay out the new ground rules are described below.

Guidelines for New Ground Rules

Creating new ground rules is the software update. You are creating a new relationship between your client and his or her negative self-talk. It is a great process with a few guidelines:

- The new rules give your client the power to dismiss the inner critic at will.

- After your client tells the inner critic the new ground rules, the inner critic may balk, argue, throw a fit, etc. The point is to envision how the inner critic will react when your client tells it that it is no longer in charge. It does not matter how the inner critic will react. Your client is not to engage, but simply distract the inner critic with milk and cookies (or some other creative distraction) and get on with life!

- The new ground rules can be silly and fun.

Here are some powerful questions about the inner critic: (Ideally, replace the words "inner critic" with the nickname that your client creates.)

- When does your inner critic show up most often?

- What is its mission?

- What does your inner critic want for you?

- What do you want your inner critic to know?

The inner critic exercise clears the negative self-talk out of the path, and the future-self exercise fills the gap with a stellar, positive mental structure.

When explaining the *Inner Critic* exercise to parents, I use the following definition: "The Inner Critic is the personification of useless self-talk. The exercise is designed for students to both recognize negative self-talk and have a simple, easy structure to distance themselves from it."

I strongly recommend doing the *Inner Critic* before the *Future-Self* exercise, although the two work well in the same session. The *Inner Critic* exercise clears the negative self-talk out of the path, and the *Future-Self* fills the gap with a stellar, positive mental structure.

Chapter 19: Powerful Relationships

Questions to Consider

Powerful Relationships

- What earlier exercise does *Powerful Relationships* build upon?

- What is the structure of the *Powerful Relationships* chart?

- What is that "magic leap" clients make half way through creating their first powerful relationship chart?

Powerful Relationships

powerful |ˈpou(-ə)rfəl|

adjective
having great power or strength.
• (of a person, organization, or country) having control and influence over people and events.
• having a strong effect on people's feelings or thoughts.
ORIGIN Middle English : from Anglo-Norman French *poeir*, from an alteration of Latin *posse 'be able.'*

relationship |riˈlā sh ən ͵ sh ip|

noun
the way in which two or more concepts, objects, or people are connected, or the state of being connected.
• the way in which two or more people or organizations regard and behave toward each other.
ORIGIN mid 16th cent.: from Latin *relat- 'brought back,'* from the verb *referre* (see refer).

What

Powerful Relationships is an exercise that uses life coaching principles to help clients understand the assumptions that they are making in their relationships and create well-designed actions to improve them. It is a chance for a coach to help the client proactively. It is important for clients to be reminded that they cannot control the thoughts, habits, and actions of others; they can only control their own. However, when clients learn to manage their own thoughts and assumptions about others, it can greatly influence the relationship. This exercise can be found in the *Academic Life Coaching Workbook*. The three elements of creating powerful relationships are:

- **The client's choice.** In life coaching, the client drives the agenda. If a client wants to focus on a specific relationship, this is an outstanding tool to do so. Often, clients want to have a better relationship with someone, but at the same time, they also want to protect themselves from being hurt. The client has the choice to change his or her assumptions while still maintaining the bubble of protection. In short, this exercise only works if the client is willing to take personal responsibility for their role in the relationship and *chooses* to put in the effort to improve it.

- **The assumptions that the client makes about people.** The exercise shows how simple, yet challenging, it can be to change assumptions about people. The exercise helps the client focus on her or his specific role in creating the relationship.

- **Empathy.** This exercise also accounts for the inherent nature of relationships and that the client is only one part of the equation. The exercise helps the client understand what it is like from the other person's point of view, focuses on building empathy, and uncovers resources to manage the relationship.

Why

- **Gives the client a powerful choice to improve a relationship.** Helping the client focus on improving a relationship is a key to helping him or her look at specific areas in life.

- **Focuses on the client's role.** Just like a well-designed action, powerful relationships only focus on what the client can specifically control. This exercise points out that the client can only control his or her own assumptions and actions. Focusing on those two things is the best way for the client to improve a relationship.

- **Asks clients to take a leap and think empathetically.** Essentially, the coach is asking the client to think from the point of view of the other person in the relationship. It is similar to Level Two listening and helps clients understand how they are being viewed by the other person. That leap of empathy helps to improve the situation and is often the key for this exercise to be successful.

- **Aligns assumptions.** People naturally want their assumptions to be true because they like to think they can predict the future and therefore have control over it. This exercise helps clients align their assumptions with the other person's actions and wants.

How

The charts in the *Academic Life Coaching Workbook* are surprisingly simple. There are just two charts and a prompt for your client to explore an assumption that is not working. The goal is for them to change it into one that does work. Explain that there is a transition from looking at who your client is as a person to her or his leadership abilities, who he or she is in relationships, and his or her impact on the community.

1) If you are seeing a relationship issue pop-up a lot in coaching, invite your client to further explore what is not working in the relationship.

2) Have your client write down some assumptions about the other person in the relationship.

3) After your client has written some negative assumptions ask, "If you were to act from those assumptions, what actions would you take on that person?"

4) Follow the prompts around the *Powerful Relationships* Chart in the *Academic Life Coaching Workbook*.

5) Repeat the same series, "What assumptions?" then "What actions?" for the other person, based on the actions that your client takes.

6) Then, point out that those actions that the other person takes will likely confirm the original negative assumptions that your client has about the other person.

7) Look for patterns in this one assumption and relationship that occur in other areas of your client's life.

8) After you explore this area, invite your client to choose a positive assumption and apply the same process of looking at the interdependence of each person's assumptions and actions. In large part, each assumption relies on the other person also holding the same assumption and actions. If your client breaks the old cycle and can successfully stay in the new cycle so the momentum of the relationship can move in a different direction, your client has mastered the art of building a powerful relationship.

9) You may need to remind your client that he or she does not necessarily have to believe in the positive assumption yet. It can be difficult for a client to create a positive assumption about another person when the relationship needs improvement. The point of the exercise is not to force your client to believe the positive assumption. The point is for the client to gain awareness of how changing the assumption may impact the relationship.

10) Observe the cycle and put your coaching skills to use. You've created a coaching rich environment to bring growth and value to the session.

Leadership starts with knowing yourself and building relationships with others. *Powerful Relationships* build on the personal growth and transformation that your client has undergone up to this point. The next stage is to apply the newly learned concepts in your client's own life to how she or he relates and communicates with others. This exercise applies the concept of the *Assumption Chart* to relationships. Students have found it useful for parents, teachers, and friends.

This exercise works because it takes the emotional charge out of relationships that are not functioning very well. Simply changing an assumption about someone does not magically make the relationship better. However, it helps set the stage for clients to get out of their own way and feel less of a negative emotional charge in order to build powerful relationships.

This exercise can put students in a reflective mood. The nature of the exercise gives them the responsibility for making their relationships strong. That responsibility is empowering, but it can also be daunting. Sometimes students will even experience an energy dip as they process what they are learning. This is perfectly normal and a good sign that you're facilitating some major internal work. I often like to check in with my client a day or two after the exercise to see how things are going. This is big, important work, and this session is extremely powerful.

Chapter 20: Empathy

Questions to Consider

Building Empathy

- What does the *Building Empathy* exercise pinpoint from the earlier *Powerful Relationships* exercise?

- Why do we recommend using you, the coach, as the example model for your client's empathy?

- Why is the *Building Empathy* exercise so powerful?

Building Empathy

empathy |ˈempəTHē|

noun

the ability to understand and share the feelings of another.
ORIGIN early 20th cent.: from Greek *empatheia* (from *em-* '*in*' + *pathos* '*feeling*') translating German *Einfühlung* .

The previous exercise encourages students to take responsibility for their assumptions in relationships. This exercise empowers them to take *leadership* in those relationships. The *Building Empathy* exercise can be found in the *Academic Life Coaching Workbook*, just after *Powerful Relationships*. Empathy is one of the core elements of emotional intelligence. Building it can sometimes be a challenge, but the first step is helping your client experience empathy directly in your coaching relationship.

Much of what we do as coaches is based on empathy. I have spent whole sessions entirely empathetic, only realizing later that, "Oh, yeah, I'm here too." Such sessions feel great. It's as if a whole new world opens up, and you're completely at the service of someone else.

Exploring this concept with a student aims to give a clear glimpse of that same awareness of empathy. As a life coach, you are allowing the roles to switch momentarily. You are asking your client to be empathetic *with you* sitting across the table. It's an unusual exercise because young people usually don't venture guesses about what it's really like to be older or what it's really like to be an adult. Because you're sitting right there, your client's guesses suddenly become real. Those guesses are going to be judged for accuracy (at first), and your job as a coach is to encourage your client to make those guesses and explore using imagination to enhance empathy.

By temporarily switching who is actively empathetic (you or your client), you've created an experience that leads to a coaching-rich environment. The next step is to resume the role as coach and ask your client about the experience. Ask your client what opportunities are available to apply empathy. Empathy gives designed actions a powerful boost.

What

- **Permission to do an unusual exercise.** Asking permission is a useful tool that empowers clients to partner with you in the design of the coaching session. Asking permission is a useful frame for unusual exercises or ones that require your client to take risks and try out something new.

- **Role reversal.** This exercise requires the client to do Level Two listening with you for a period of time. Such a switch gives your client the direct experience of empathy, which is useful for the rest of the coaching exercise.

- **Curiosity and action.** During the exercise, you use your skills, become curious, and create action steps informed by empathy.

Why

- **Creates direct experience.** By asking your client to be empathic with you, your client has a direct experience of empathy. Such a fresh experience provides many opportunities for you to create learning and increased self-awareness for your client.

- **Is applicable to other areas.** Empathy is such a useful skill for people to change perspectives, communicate effectively, and step up powerfully into leadership. The skill used on the micro level with just one person can also be applied to other areas of your client's life.

How

1) Introduce the concept of empathy. (Here's the quick difference between compassion and empathy. Compassion is feeling sympathetic pity and concern for the sufferings or misfortunes of others. Empathy is the ability to understand and share the feelings of others.)

2) Explain that the exercise involves switching roles for a few minutes. You are asking your client to be empathetic with you, the coach. The purpose is for the client to get a feeling for what it is like to be

empathetic with someone sitting directly across (or on the other side of the phone) from himself or herself.

3) Ask permission from your client to use the exercise.

4) Sometimes I introduce the concepts of levels of listening, then encourage my client to take a risk in venturing guesses about what my life is like. What do I care about the most? What are my fears? My hopes? My dreams? My expectations?

5) Allow your client to guess. Give feedback if it feels natural.

6) Diffuse judgment. The important thing is that your client feels like they are flexing their empathy muscle.

7) Switch roles back. Go back to you being the empathetic coach focused on your client. Ask your client about what the empathetic experience was like. What worked well? What was hard about it? What was easy about it? What did it feel like when you had to guess at first? What surprised you about your imagination?

8) Ask questions about how it felt using Level One listening (for the sake of self) vs. Level Two (for the sake of other).

9) Apply the learning.

10) Then follow the prompts in the *Academic Life Coaching Workbook* to do a similar guessing and exploration of empathy for someone else in your client's life. Parents and teachers are popular choices.

Chapter 21: Passion

Questions to Consider

Identifying Your Passions

- What is the challenge for students to identify an interest as a passion?

- What is the difference between the subject and process of a passion?

Identifying Your Passions

passion |ˈpaSHən|

noun
1 strong and barely controllable emotion: *a man of impetuous passion*.
• a state or outburst of strong emotion: oratory in which he gradually works himself up into a passion.
• an intense desire or enthusiasm for something: *the English have a passion for gardens*.
• a thing arousing enthusiasm: modern furniture is a particular passion of Bill's.
ORIGIN Middle English: from Old French, from late Latin *passio(n-)* (chiefly a term in Christian theology), from Latin *pati 'suffer.'*

Often referred to in graduation speeches – either lauded or regarded as overrated – passion typically means those much loved pursuits, internal drives, and lifelong desires. Let's go old school on the definition of passion for a moment. It comes from the Latin word *patior,* which means *to suffer*. In the hands of a skilled Academic Life Coach, passion is something that your client is willing to pursue even in the face of suffering. Why? Because the whole process – the successes, the failures, the learning, the journey – is worth it.

I love this session. It comes in *Academic Life Coaching Program*. By now, you know your client well, and your client knows you. It's valuable to explore any special interests or talents that your client may not think important. For instance, so many clients with whom I work have idiosyncratic interests: building and racing remote control model cars, designing men's shoes, the *Harry Potter* game of Quidditch, or tracking real-estate sales. Often, students don't think much of these pursuits, yet they can offer clues to buried passions.

Similar to the distinction between a content value and a process value, the initial exploration of an interest can uncover these deeper passions. When you have found something your client cares about enough to take bold action and recover from mistakes, you've found passion. Align that passion with a need in the community, and you've got the path to develop a young leader. This exercise attempts to ground students in an awareness of passion, while the following concepts in the *Academic Life Coaching Program* nurture that passion with action steps.

What

- **Clarifying passions by exploring interests.** The *Academic Life Coaching Workbook* gives students a few prompts to explore concepts that spark awareness of their interests and passions.

- **Making a distinction between a topic and a process.** This is exactly like the difference between a topic and a process value (Chapter 15, ALC Client Session 5). You can draw the same kind of differences for passions. Practically speaking, not much separates a value from a passion, other than the intensity of pursuit. People tend to pursue passions more than values, but in function, both concepts are extremely similar.

- **Acknowledgment that the pain is worth it.** Using the old school definition of passion as experiencing something painful, you help your client prepare for doing hard things, building resilience, and improving their endurance to keep going when challenged.

Why

- **Relates to grit.** Grit is the ability to keep moving forward when the going gets tough. Recently, scholars and educators have lauded grit as perhaps the single most important skill that leads to success. Helping students identify something worth fighting for helps them build grit. Having a clearly defined passion prepares people mentally to expect, and even welcome, obstacles.

- **Promotes action.** Doing the work to understand a passion makes it easier to identify which action to pursue. People like what they understand. Making a passion more understandable makes the required action more acceptable. Try it. The human mind is wired to encourage flow, and a big part of flow is playing in the area between complete understanding and slight confusion. Making the slightly confusing understandable is another definition of learning. Crafting a slightly vague interest into a crystal clear passion mimics the brain's circuitry of learning and flow. Amazing actions and results happen when engaged in flow.

How

1) Introduce the idea of passion as something worth doing even when things get hard.

2) Go through the prompts and become curious about what your client loves to do and why.

3) A favorite question is: "Are you interested in anything that is considered odd or unusual?" This question often elicits great clues to passions. Sometimes there is nothing there, but if there is, then it's usually a great place to explore.

   Other questions about passion:

   - What do you love to do and why do you love doing it?

   - What activities give you purpose?

   - If you had a month completely free of obligations, what would you pursue?

   - What would you pursue if you were guaranteed to succeed?

   - What are you honoring when you pursue this passion?

4) This exercise is straightforward. The coaching homework usually focuses on being more curious about what makes you love your passion so much.

Chapter 22: Leadership

Questions to Consider

Leadership Projects

- What is the recommended timeframe for a student's leadership project? During the academic year? During the summer?

Leadership Styles with Core Motivation

- Why look at *Core Motivation* now in the context of leadership and passion?

Mission Statements

- What is a mission statement?
- What is the recommended timeframe for a mission statement?
- What is the purpose of a mission statement?

Leadership Projects

leadership |ˈlēdərˌSHip|

noun
the action of leading a group of people or an organization: *different styles of leadership.*
• the state or position of being a leader: *the leadership of the party.*
• [treated as sing. or pl.] the leaders of an organization, country, etc.: *a change of leadership had become desirable.*

leader |ˈlēdər|

noun
1 the person who leads or commands a group, organization, or country: *the leader of a protest group.*
• an organization or company that is the most advanced or successful in a particular area: *a leader in the use of video conferencing.*
• (also Leader of the House)Brit. a member of the government officially responsible for initiating business in Parliament.

So often leadership is an amorphous concept that does not really mean much to students. Is being on student council leadership? How about being the head of the foreign language club? Community service? Those leadership positions are not what we will be discussing in this section. Instead, this brand of leadership is mission-specific (what do you want to create or accomplish?) and project oriented (what are you actually going to do?).

The foundation of leadership is not about convincing others to believe in what your client believes. It's about deciding to step up and pursue something that your client wholeheartedly believes is worth pursuing. So, which comes first in making an effective leader: the push to step up or the raw talent of the leader? This is our version of the chicken and the egg conundrum. The short answer is *the push*. Coaching is based on the theory that establishing a vision and taking action steps develops talent. It's a growth-oriented mindset. Such an approach assumes that, if there is desire and push, clients will develop the necessary skills, perspectives, or mindset shifts to gain the vital experiences they need to become great leaders.

The following leadership exercise is designed to get students thinking about what projects would be exciting to complete. It is designed to get clients thinking about ways they can take what they are learning and begin to support others. The *Leadership Projects* exercise can be found in the *Academic Life Coaching Workbook*. A leadership practice simply involves thinking intentionally about the needs and opportunities to serve and putting in place small, consistent steps that align with the client's personal growth. Current skill level doesn't matter yet. The first step is establishing a clear and exciting vision. This can start with the question "what need do you see in your community?" Then, "what kind of impact do you want to have?" The next question is "what small step (or big step!) can you take to fill that need?"

By activating this desire and vision, students design their projects and learn to lead. These projects also design the students. By asking "what's needed now?" and "how can I best serve?" the project dictates the skills and experience needed to move forward. The project designs the leader as the leader undertakes the project.

The *Academic Life Coaching Program* adopts a service-based leadership model. A leader is someone who serves others, creates experiences, and builds relationships. By stepping into the role of a leader, students naturally develop the habit and skill of being proactive. Being a leader is a transformative act that has positive impacts in all other areas of life.

What

- **The need.** The leadership practice starts with your client identifying a need that she or he sees in his or her support system or community. This may be as simple as a person in your client's life who needs encouragement or as complex as designing a program to meet important needs in the community.

- **The desire.** The crux of leadership is identifying where that need meets your client's desire to take action.

- **Tangible steps.** Once the need and the desire are clear, tangible steps are necessary to realize the leadership project.

Why

- **Projects stretch leadership.** By encouraging projects for students to accomplish outside the bounds of school, you are asking them to be proactive and stretch their leadership skills.

- **Effort leads to outcomes.** By focusing on effort that the client can control, you help clients focus on separating their abilities from the results. Whether the outcomes happen quickly or not, clients will benefit from focusing on the growth they can control and the mindsets they are able to build. When students put in enough effort, outcomes follow.

- **Actions and learning go beyond the Academic Life Coaching Program.** The ALC program is designed to end after ten sessions. The leadership project, and all of the learning and tangible steps it will require, will continue to engage students in learning and stretch their skills beyond the *Academic Life Coaching Program*. The project becomes the teacher, giving students valuable, practical experience in getting things done.

How

1) Explain the concept of developing a leadership practice. Say something like "as you have grown through the coaching process and learned to adopt a growth mindset, one powerful outcome is to share that with others. The concept of a leadership practice can provide a framework to determine how you want to be a leader to others and it continues to engage your own growth mindset. What are your thoughts?"

2) Follow the prompts in the *Academic Life Coaching Workbook*.

3) Look for life coaching opportunities to create learning and increased self-awareness.

4) The workbook has space for two projects. It's useful to go through the process of brainstorming and working through two different projects so your client can experience the process twice. Learning the process and how to plan out the project are just as important (and maybe even more important over time) as completing the project. This could include anything from encouraging text messages to developing a program. Arrange these goals from simple to complex, allowing your client to see that the ideas they traditionally think of as leadership ideas are achieved by starting small.

5) If your client has big ideas for programs or projects, take time to explore their vision and future plans. What are they motivated to

accomplish? How does that motivation translate into making challenging decisions right now?

6) Finally, take time to hone in on 1-2 actions your client is motivated to take this week. Then ask follow-up questions. What are they most excited about? How will this move them towards other leadership opportunities? What additional lessons do they expect to learn in the process?

7) Well-designed actions are really important in this session. Be sure to identify one or two that are relatively easy to complete in a week. As an Academic Life Coach, it's helpful to create momentum in the initial phases of undertaking the project. Even mini-projects are useful here. The focus isn't as much on creating a grand project, as it is giving your client the experience of action-based service leadership.

As the coach, it's helpful to recognize that the concept of a leadership practice is more about your client continuing to develop the growth mindset rather than accomplishing large tasks or achieving great success. Supporting your clients in thinking intentionally about their own growth and fostering leadership by helping them share it with others will serve them well in the end.

Leadership Styles with Core Motivation

What

Throughout the *Academic Life Coaching Program,* students explore personal growth and learning. Yet, the *Core Motivation* tool is especially powerful in isolating a client's being or core characteristics. Starting with the introductory interview, the client experiences *Core Motivation*, which develops a deeper understanding of his or her personality. The client then starts using a framework to leverage strengths and overcome weaknesses.

After completing seven out of the ten *Academic Life Coaching Program's* sessions, you have developed a strong relationship with your client. You are aware of your client's strengths and weaknesses and you have insights into possible directions your client can explore.

With this background, it makes sense to revisit *Core Motivation* through the lens of how your client can specifically build on the strengths of his or her personality. The *Leadership Styles with Core Motivation* exercise can be found in the *Academic Life Coaching Workbook*. By looking at personality through the leadership lens, you can help your client take those next steps in personal development and push performance to the next level.

- **Definition of leadership.** There are many different definitions of leadership. From a coaching point of view, leadership starts with the ability to lead yourself, to do something that you believe in, and to build effective and powerful relationships with others.

- **Core motivation tool.** *Core Motivation* consists of nine personality types. By this point in the ALC Program, you and your client are very clear on which one or two types best describe your client. If needed, you can refer back to the tool and charts in the introductory session.

- **Exploring strengths and weaknesses.** Included in the *Academic Life Coaching Workbook* is a table of typical strengths and weaknesses from the perspective of leadership for each of the nine *Core Motivation* personality types. You can use the chart to create and deepen learning and clarity for your client.

- **New direction.** With increased clarity and deepened learning, you can help your client determine new directions of action. Using the frame of personality strengths and weaknesses, you are giving your client a foundation to explore action steps that will spark an upward spiral of increased leadership. This develops skill and ability to take on increasingly challenging projects.

Why

- **Focuses on being from the leadership perspective.** The natural focus on a client pushing himself or herself past previous personal performance boundaries is the reason why *Core Motivation* combined with leadership is so powerful. Such a strengths-focused discussion gives your clients a deeper sense of resilience and taps into intrinsic motivation for the sake of self-realization. Developing ourselves is intensely enjoyable and helps us take on increasingly difficult challenges because we experience a sense of accomplishment and greater capacity to do hard things.

- **Revisits a recurring theme.** The *Academic Life Coaching Program* starts with your client exploring his or her *Core Motivation*. This session revisits that exploration. By continuing the theme of addressing personality strengths and weaknesses, you increase the chances that your client will remember and use the tool even after the ALC program completes. Coming back to the *Core Motivation* tool periodically through the coaching relationship mimics spaced practice sessions, which has been proven to increase long-term working memory.

- **Leverages personality as a tool.** The *Leadership Styles with Core Motivation* exercise prepares students to take the next leadership step in service of a larger mission. It's designed to get your client thinking about personality as a tool that can help her or him pursue a passion and step into leadership. The purpose is to align your client's passion and natural talent with an eye to the future. How might she or he apply a passion and talent to a leadership project in the community?

How

1) Explore the "Leadership Styles with *Core Motivation*" material in the *Academic Life Coaching Workbook*.

2) Ask your client curious questions based on using personality strengths in service of pursuing a passion.

3) Ask your client about potential blind spots and weaknesses.

4) Design action steps to explore and hone a personality strength.

Mission Statements

mission |ˈmiSHən|

noun
1 an important assignment carried out for political, religious, or commercial purposes, typically involving travel: *a trade mission to Mexico.*
     Mission comes from the Latin misere meaning *to be sent.*
2 a strongly felt aim, ambition, or calling: his main mission in life has been to cut unemployment.
ORIGIN mid 16th cent. (denoting the sending of the Holy Spirit into the world): from Latin missio(n-), from mittere 'send.'

What

So which comes first – the leadership project or the mission statement? Typically, the mission statement comes before the leadership project plan. I used to ask students to first create a mission statement and then design a leadership project. However, something interesting happened when I circled back around and visited the mission statement *after* the leadership project. Clients would get reconnected to the deeper purpose and come up with a more creative name for the mission statement. This took pressure off trying to craft an overarching mission statement, which put pressure on coming up with a brilliant project.

By using the lens of a specific project, the *Mission Statement* exercise provides a natural limit or boundary to the mission statement. It can be found just after the *Leadership Proj*ects exercise in the *Academic Life Coaching Workbook.* Such a boundary is tremendously useful in removing pressure from the mission statement needing to be an over-arching, this-is-my-one-and-only-life-purpose sentence that captures every facet of my being.

The mission statement is a concise sentence that identifies aspirations and is easy to reference throughout the day. It aligns action with intention. It guides decision-making. A simple, powerful mission statement has the power to influence major life decisions, helping students determine the best action to take based on a larger vision. A mission statement has these three characteristics:

- **Short, sweet, and to the point.** Your mission is what you are sent to do. A mission statement is a short sentence, usually 10 words or less, that captures the purpose of the leadership project. Short, sweet, and to the point, a mission statement speaks to both the action and the desired outcome.

- **Inspiring.** Another quality of mission statements is the motivation they inspire. You know you have created an outstanding mission statement when it inspires you and others to take bold action.

- **Guide for action.** At its best, a mission statement guides decision making. A simple, powerful mission statement has the power to influence major life decisions as well as help guide day-to-day decisions based on a larger vision. For example, the mission of Academic Life Coaching is *to revolutionize education*. It guides our thinking as a company: who to reach out to, what projects to take on next, what company culture to create, and how to design our coach training sessions. A mission statement for a student could be *to optimize learning*. The actions could range from always using a planner to being strict about study sessions.

Why

- **Powerfully communicates.** A strong mission statement helps others understand why your client is taking on the project. Such communication makes it easier for your client to express a vision quickly, which is an important element of being an effective leader.

- **Provides focus.** A strong mission statement provides focus for your client. Especially in a world filled with distractions, having a clear, short-term mission statement can be extremely powerful in helping clients tone down the outside noise. This increased focus facilitates clients' more productive accomplishment of well-designed actions. Accomplished missions lead to a powerful cycle of accomplishment along with stamina and skill, which leads to better outcomes. The positive cycle of accomplishment and effort is set in motion, and a strong mission statement provides the focus for the process to continue.

- **Inspires motivation.** Mission statements add a level of importance and fun to projects, which helps clients tap into intrinsic and proactive motivation.

How

1) Introduce the concept of mission statements. Use some examples in your own life. My current mission (and one that I've been implementing for over seven years) is to *redesign education*. It's short, yet effective. I often ask myself, "Will this help me redesign education?" "What needs to happen next to support my mission?"

2) Using the leadership project as a guide, go through the prompts and have your client create short, useful mission statements.

3) I usually give my clients some coaching homework. For instance, they can bring their mission statement to mind one or more times a day. Some great homework will also result from the leadership project and the planning involved in undertaking it. I try to integrate the two exercises together.

Chapter 23: Celebration and Resilience

Questions to Consider

Resilience

- Looking back over the course of the *Academic Life Coaching Program*, what has worked well for you?

- What kind of system can you create going forward?

- Why is resilience so important?

Celebration

- What makes a successful celebration?

- Why is it important to take time to celebrate?

Resilience Intelligence

resilience |riˈzilyəns|

noun
1 the ability of a substance or object to spring back into shape; elasticity: *nylon is excellent in wearability and resilience.*
2 the capacity to recover quickly from difficulties; toughness: *the often remarkable resilience of so many British institutions.*

Resilience is derived from the Latin word *re-,* which means *back-and-forth,* and *silere,* which means *to dance.* Resilience is literally "dancing back." As a metaphor of dancing, resilience is brilliant. We each need challenges in our lives to bring out the best in us. As the metaphor suggests, being resilient is not about being so tough as to not bend, but rather a flexible, almost rhythmic experience of finding a way to bounce back from a setback, hopefully with a little style.

One of the foundational ideas in the *Academic Life Coaching Program* is the mindset of welcoming those setbacks as opportunities to grow. When a student adopts a perspective of accepting failure as part of a larger process, creativity and motivation naturally grow stronger. In this chapter, we focus on resilience as an invitation to adopt a strong growth-mindset and explore your client's relationship to setbacks and rekindling motivation.

This chapter explores the idea of learned resilience; an intelligence associated with being resilient. The concept emerged from hundreds of hours of coaching and seeing similar patterns emerge among people who have been successful. Some people seem to have tapped into a certain instinct that helps them thrive under stress, and even welcome hard work and preparation. Such an instinct is rooted in the same mechanisms that promote survival, from playing, learning, and practicing to establishing relationships beyond immediate family.

As an intelligence, there appears to be certain choices that lead to increased resilience.[1] The more likely someone is to choose the more resilient choice, the higher their resilience intelligence. This chapter offers a tour through the factors that contribute to resilience, such as internal mindsets, habits, and the strength of

---

1 A good starting point for learning more about resilience can be found in Angela Duckworth's original research and her book. See:
  o Duckworth, Angela, and James J. Gross. "Self-Control and Grit: Related but Separable Determinants of Success." Current directions in psychological science 23.5 (2014): 319–325.
  o Duckworth, Angela. Grit: the power of passion and perseverance. New York, Scribner, 2016.

external support networks. Resilience is built by believing in oneself as well as having healthy, meaningful relationships in our lives. Like dancing, being resilient requires a good dance partner. If we are going to stretch the metaphor even more, having a great DJ and scene also helps in setting the energy of the room and finding a groove. It takes both an individual and a village to be resilient.

The following looks at the factors of resilience intelligence. The primary source comes from interviews with students who had a remarkable improvement in grades from one semester to the next, adults who bounced back from setbacks in career or financial challenges, and clients who achieved inspiring health goals from lifestyle change to recovery from injury. Supporting sources include the Kübler-Ross model of the five stages of grief, Diane Coutu's *How Resilience Works*, and a review of supporting research, which also underlines the value of having supportive relationships.

At this point in the program, your client has committed to a number of well-designed actions. He or she has taken those first few steps towards putting together a larger project. No doubt, your client has experienced success and setbacks.

Avoid the notion that each concept in the *Academic Life Coaching Program* is equally important for your client. Certain concepts will be more useful than others. Your job is to help your client identify those moments when the tide turned away from despair to motivation. The temptation is to equate motivation or success with the results. Results do matter. As an Academic Life Coach, you are looking for those concepts that help your client move forward and learn, especially when outside circumstances were not offering much extrinsic motivation. Those are the golden ideas and concepts for your client. Identifying them and helping your client design them into systems is priceless. The *Resilience* exercise is in the *Academic Life Coaching Workbook*.

What

Resilience is as much a cycle as it is a series of individual traits and the strength of our external resources. The cycle starts with a challenge, with its mixture of acute and chronic aspects. In many ways, the degree of the challenge and its match or mismatch to an individual's skills or resources function like the psychology of flow. Too little challenge leads to boredom. Too much challenge leads to being overwhelmed. People often emerge stronger, more fulfilled, and more grateful for having dealt with a surmountable challenge. Indeed, it seems that having such challenges in life is a pathway to realizing more of our potential and pushes us to places we never considered possible. Human beings were designed to be resilient. The following are the factors that increase resilience.

Foundation of Resilience

These are the two most important elements of resilience intelligence that need to be developed before a big challenge arrives: 1) the strength & resources of a network and 2) belief in one's ability to meet the challenge.

1) **Relationships: Strength & Resources of the Network.** One of the aspects that separates resilience from a simple character trait is the inclusion of relationships and available outside resources as a major factor of resilience. Relationships that empower individuals and offer useful resources to meet challenges help individuals be more resilient. When looking at college student retention or engagement, one of the major factors is the presence or absence of a meaningful, mentor relationship between a student and a professor or advisor on campus. Parents, relatives, church community, coworkers, friends, counselors, and coaches can all provide support and boost resilience when needed. The key factors are strength, number of connections, and the quality of support offered. Support that cares, listens, and can provide tangible resources such as money, information, or empowerment help individuals to be more resilient. The resilient choice is for people to seek and nurture supportive relationships and to ask for help early and often. The usual challenge to asking for help is a belief in rugged individualism, and sometimes, a cultural belief that asking for help means weakness or failure. However, support is essential to success. Key question: To what degree have you built your support network?

2) **Belief in the ability to meet the challenge.** The more one believes in their ability to meet the challenge or eventually learn the skills to meet the challenge, the more likely they are to embody resilience intelligence. It requires a mindset that sees most challenges as temporary and trusts that healing will happen, even through aspects of the challenge that are permanent and painful. The beauty of such

optimism is that it initially does not need to be the optimism of the individual. For example, a coach, therapist, or friend might initially see the opportunity and be supportively optimistic. It helps to have someone in our lives who sees our brilliance and believes in us more than we do. However, for it to have a long-term effect on resilience intelligence, the individual must adopt such an optimistic view. Such a belief to meet future challenges also relies on an individual's beliefs on potential and talent. Referencing Carol Dweck's work on growth versus fixed mindsets, the less resilient choice is believing that potential is fixed, leading to approaching each challenge as a test of talent. The more resilient choice is seeing potential as a by-product of effort, and approaching challenges as opportunities to learn and gain more skills.[2] Key question: Do you believe that you can work through and learn from a challenge?

---

[2] For more information on Carol Dweck's research on the importance of mindset, see Dweck, Carol S. Mindset: The New Psychology Of Success. New York : Ballantine Books, 2008.

Stages of Resilience

1) **Acceptance: Willingness and ability to assess the full scope of the challenge.** Coutu, in *How Resilience Works,* starts by looking at an individual's ability to accurately assess the difficulty of the situation. It takes tremendous courage to look at the full scope of a tough situation. In assessing a situation, a slightly pessimistic perspective, surprisingly, is the more resilient choice. The opposite is an unwillingness or inability to look at a challenge and to underestimate the resources or effort required to succeed. It seems that resilience picks up where the cycle of grief leaves off. After someone has gone through denial, anger, bargaining, and depression, he or she finally reaches the stage of acceptance. With the first two elements of resilience established, acceptance marks the first stage of working through a challenge. Key question: What is the full scope of the challenge?

2) **Responsibility: Ownership of the future outcome of the situation.** Looking at what went wrong is useful in gathering information to make decisions moving forward, but dwelling in regret or stewing in revenge drains precious resources and creates obstacles to resilience. This factor does not discount the pain and hurt that victims can feel. Instead, it points to an aspect of humanity that is able to rise above horrific actions or situations, transcend victimhood, and take on the responsibility for future actions. Healing from the past and taking ownership of future outcomes empowers an individual to use more of his or her energy to solve the current problem. Building on concepts from Positive Psychology such as *Broaden and Build,* leads to being proactive, creative, and adding more resources beyond what is immediately offered. Responsibility is the fourth element of resilience and the second major step towards overcoming a challenge. Key question: To what degree are you taking responsibility for the future outcome?

3) **Determination: Where there is a why, there is a way.** The hard truth: not every task or goal is worth the effort to grit it out. Sometimes the wiser choice is to find something else to pursue. Doing something "just because" or without much thought about other options or choices, does not lead to resilience. However, if the goal is worth it, taking the

extra step of having an articulated purpose for a worthwhile goal is one of the factors of resilience intelligence. Intrinsic or empathetic motivations (doing something for the sake of someone else or for a larger cause) are usually more lasting than conditional motivation (doing something for the sake of a reward). The quality of the motivation is determined by its ability to provide an empowering perspective and spark action, even in the face of setbacks. Determination to keep moving forward marks the third stage of becoming successfully resilient. Key questions: Why are you pursuing this goal? How compelling is that reason when things do not go your way?

The Path of Recovery

1) **Troubleshooting: Creativity matters and feedback is gold.** The next stage is marked by troubleshooting. People in this stage start gathering more information and resources, trying out ideas, and welcoming feedback. Creativity and persistence to keep trying out new ideas are hallmarks of this stage. The more an individual can be creative and develop shorter, more frequent feedback loops, the higher the resilience intelligence. For example, imagine someone trying to recover from injury. The more feedback gathered – from designing several measures during a therapy session to measuring results daily – the higher chance of using that information to make better future decisions. The less resilient choice is to procrastinate and put off action or do it once, then stop if the feedback is negative. The more resilient choice is to set up a series of mini-experiments and learn from each trial run, expecting to receive information on how to make or do it better. Troubleshooting and creativity mark the fourth stage of resilience. Key question: How do you gather feedback to try out new ideas?

2) **Gratitude: What doesn't kill you makes you stronger.** The final stage of resilience is the growth and adaptation to meet the challenge accompanied with a sense of relief, happiness and gratitude. The setbacks experienced in life develop some of the best qualities and help push potential further than previously thought possible. The

learning that occurred and stamina developed to meet challenges translates to a deeper belief in one's abilities to meet future setbacks. The whole cycle feeds an individual's sense of self and ability and creates a cycle of ever-increasing skill sets designed to take on future problems.

Why

- **Everyone can build resilience intelligence.** Human beings are naturally resilient. Knowing what factors actually help build resilience gives people a better awareness of which to focus on and where someone is at in the steps of resilience. If there is a step missing, it is often difficult to get to the next stage in the process.

- **Focused questions.** The stages of resilience point out different aspects that you can address with your client. Explore which stage your client is currently in and which stage is coming next.

- **Importance of asking for help.** So many times, people do not reach out for help or use the resources available due to a mistaken belief in rugged individuality, embarrassment, or misplaced pride. Building relationships and tapping networks for resources is one of the most useful actions to take both before and during a setback.

- **Frames setbacks as temporary.** By helping clients recognize failure or procrastination as part of a larger structure included in troubleshooting, they avoid the trap of believing they are somehow flawed. Clients feel prepared to keep moving forward rather than dwelling on past setbacks.

- **Builds plans based on past success.** The magic of the session comes from helping your client develop a plan for the future in the face of a challenge. Helping your client recover from procrastination or lack of action allows him or her to develop more resilience. The habit of embracing harder and harder challenges builds a greater capacity to bounce back from setbacks.

How

1) Ask your client to look at a goal he or she wants to work on. Use the Resilience Chart to help your client create a visual of his or her resilience structure.

2) Use the resilience intelligence chart as you would an assessment wheel. Go through the seven elements in the section above to create an initial assessment. Have your client rate his or herself on a scale of 1 to 10 in each of the areas of the chart. Here is each area's description:

- **Strength of Network (Asking for Help).** The strength of community asks your client to assess how supportive others are in his or her life. It's your client's ability to build a strong support network and gather the resources necessary to withstand setbacks.

  - Key question: How have you worked to build your support network?

- **Belief in Ability to Meet the Challenge (Growth Mindset).** Whether you think you can be successful or not has a huge impact on motivation, stress levels, and ability to get into flow. This area assesses what your client thinks about his or her ability to be successful.

  - Key question: To what degree to you believe that you can work through and learn from a challenge?

- **Clarity and Acceptance of the Challenge.** While being optimistic about belief in ability is helpful, being realistic about the difficulty of the challenge is also crucial to resilience. Over optimism can derail projects and lead to disappointment. This area asks your client to look at his or her willingness to accept that the project is going to be challenging and to accept the challenge as part of the deal. Thinking that things will be a "piece of cake" is the antitheses to the kind of thinking necessary to be resilient in the long run.

  - Key question: What is the full scope of the challenge?

- **Ownership (Responsibility for the Outcome).** Blaming others or the situation short circuits resilience. Taking responsibility even for things outside your complete control leads to more resilience. It's the mindset of accepting and preparing a plan to address the situation when things go wrong.

  - Key question: How are you taking responsibility for the future outcome?

- **Determination and Clarity of Purpose.** The quality of your purpose effects the quality of your motivation and ability to keep moving when the going gets tough. This area addresses your client's clarity of purpose.

  - Key questions: Why are you pursuing this goal? How compelling is that reason when things do not go your way?

- **Troubleshooting and Gathering Feedback.** This section looks at your client's habit of gathering feedback and looking at the data available to make better decisions. Gathering feedback helps your client adjust and develop a stronger skill set.

  - Key question: How do you gather feedback to try out new ideas?

- **Gratitude for Learning and Stamina.** This final section is about being grateful even for the challenges and setbacks. When clients can get into a space of feeling grateful even when things go wrong, your client is demonstrating a high degree of resilience.

  - Key question: To what degree are you grateful even when things don't go your way?

3) After exploring the points above in the context of your client's topic, ask your client to shade in the percentage of area that corresponds to your client's 1 to 10 rating.

4) Just as you would with any other assessment wheel, explore what your client is learning from looking at him or herself with this tool.

5) Use the tool and the insights as a launching pad to refine the session agenda or explore other areas relating to resilience.

Celebration

celebration |ˌseləˈbrā sh ən|

noun
the action of marking one's pleasure at an important event or occasion by engaging in enjoyable, typically social, activity.
ORIGIN early 16th century: from Latin *celebratio(n-)*, from the verb *celebrare* (see celebrate).

What

From a life coaching perspective, celebration is about creating a reminder of a past success for present motivation. A useful celebration reminds clients that the *effort,* not just the result, is worth it. A well-designed celebration is fun and meaningful, but most importantly, it reminds your client of the value of work in the face of future challenges. When the tide turns, and the challenges loom large, having the memory of a celebration, or a token sitting on a desk or shelf, acts as a reminder that all the effort and work are worth it. The *Celebration* exercise can be found in the *Academic Life Coaching Workbook*. Celebrations should have the following elements:

- **Exploration.** Celebration starts with an exploration of the past or recognition of a successful action taken. It can also be forward focused, looking at some point in the future once a project is completed.

- **Acknowledgment.** A celebration is a recognition of success. Useful celebrations include both an acknowledgment of required work, effort, and the completion of the project. Sometimes it can be difficult for clients to celebrate if there hasn't been a huge success. Reflecting and acknowledging how far he or she has come helps further motivation.

- **Structure.** Sometimes celebrations can be an action, such as a party or going out to dinner. It can also be a structure like buying something special or memorable. It could be both. A useful celebration includes some element or structure that serves as a reminder of the success.

Why

- **Reinforces motivation styles.** Celebrations are powerful and put clients into a motivation mindset. Having such reminders of past success and hard work helps clients feel more energized and likely to take useful action and create systems.

- **Recognizes small accomplishments.** It is helpful to celebrate small things and small accomplishments with small celebrations. Celebration becomes a constantly evolving structure for an empowering belief, positive perspective, and value of hard work.

How

1) Lead your client through another *Wheel of Life* exercise.

2) Refer back to the first wheel that your client created. Compare the two. You'll stumble onto some great coaching questions in the process.

3) Identify your client's biggest accomplishments and times when she or he put in the most effort.

4) Find a way for your client to celebrate those successes and recognize hard work. Build in a feeling of excitement as well as an acknowledgment of the work that was required. Allow the celebration to act as a structure to champion your client.

Sample Dialogue

Coach: I think you have a solid plan to earn the grades you want.

Client: Thanks. It looks really good.

Coach: And it seems like you're excited about it. Ready to go?

Client: You know, I actually am. I was so frustrated about last year. This year seems different and this plan seems different.

Coach: When working a plan like this, it's useful to have an end celebration in mind to keep you focused on what you're trying to accomplish here and acknowledge all the effort that you're going to put into this. If you were to design a little celebration when you earn the grades you want, what would it be?

Client: Aside from holding the report card and seeing that I got above a 3.75, nothing that makes sense really comes to mind.

Coach: What do you think the biggest challenge is going to be?

Client: Making sure that when I get home I spend that first 15 minutes just looking over all my notes before I go off and get a snack. I know that if I can do that, everything else will be easy.

Coach: It's perfect. Your snack can be a daily mini-celebration that means you've been following through on going over your notes for 15 minutes. What would you do to mark the end of the quarter?

Client: My dad always has this tradition—whenever he has a big deal go through, he takes everyone out to dinner. It'd be great to go out to lunch with him or something.

Coach: That's perfect. When do you want to talk to your dad about it?

Client: I'll try to talk to him tonight, but it may be late. If not tonight, I'll definitely have a chance by tomorrow.

Chapter 24: Completion

Questions to Consider

Designing the Future

- What are the elements of successfully creating a plan for the future?

- Why is it important to think in terms of systems?

Completion

- What is bitter-sweet about completion?

- Why is completion important?

Designing the Future

The penultimate exercise in the *Academic Life Coaching Workbook* is about looking forward and putting all the pieces together in one giant exercise. This exercise combines creating a future vision, motivation, well-designed actions, systems, and structures. It functions as *Leadership Projects Part Two,* tweaking what students have accomplished and looking at how they can continue to use these skills moving forward. The *Designing the Future* exercise can be found in the *Academic Life Coaching Workbook*, just before its completion.

What

- **Clear vision for the future.** In the *Academic Life Coaching Workbook*, your client is prompted to think about what his or her life will be like one year from now and into the future. This gives him or her motivation for what is to come.

- **An agenda from your client.** From that vision of the future, you as a coach help your client create and identify the agenda that your client wants to focus on for the last half of the session.

- **Well-designed actions and structures for systems.** The *Academic Life Coaching Workbook* also has prompts for your client to write down ideas for well-designed actions and systems that she or he wants to create.

Why

- **Starts with the larger vision.** By starting with the larger vision, you frame the coaching conversation in a way that is meaningful and productive for your client. It also leads into the next reason this exercise is powerful – having your client set the agenda.

- **Client sets the agenda**. The main difference between coaching a high school or college student and coaching an adult is how the coach partners with the client to elicit an agenda. When working with a student, it is helpful to have a strong structure and for the coach to offer an agenda. However, a client can always change the structure or agenda based on the situation or his or her needs in the session. When working with an adult, a coach elicits the agenda completely from the client. In the *Design the Future* exercise, you as a coach lead your client through a short life coaching session in which you elicit an agenda from your client based on his or her desired area of focus. Often, it is the leadership project or something connected to a vision of the future. Other times, it is connected to immediate grades or a frustrating relationship. Whether it be grades, an upcoming test, or something related to relationships, your client has enough experience with being coached to identify appropriate agendas for a coaching session.

- **Reinforces learning with action.** Coaching works because it helps clients take meaningful action steps. It is also effective because it creates clarity, learning, and understanding. The workbook contains space for clients to write down action steps as well as the structures and systems to support actions.

How

1) Revisit your client's vision from an earlier session. It's an incredible experience for clients to reflect on a vision they made in the past and compare it to the present moment.

2) Ask powerful questions about what came true and what still needs work. Ask what they have learned about their situation and what they learned about themselves.

3) Help your client identify elements she or he might include in a future vision recording. Capturing that vision in another recording or visual representation makes for some powerful coaching homework.

4) Put elements of that vision into action, creating a well-designed action with your client.

5) Add structures and systems to support the actions.

6) There's space for three well-designed actions and systems. Having looked at resilience, then another wheel, this exercise is meant to tie

everything together and get clear on the steps forward after the program.

7) Have fun! Generating exciting and motivating ideas is always fun. You know you are coaching well if you and your client are having fun with this process.

Completion

completion |kəmˈplēSHən|

noun
the action or process of finishing something: *funds for the completion of the new building.*
• the state of being finished: work on the new golf course is nearing completion | [as modifier
] : the completion date is early next year.
ORIGIN late 15th cent.: from Latin **completion-**, from **complere** *'fill up'*

Completion is being filled up or concluded. There is an art to completing a program well. Looking at *Completion* as a skill involves mindfulness in assessing the past as well as being aware of present emotions.

A successful completion is part reflection, part acknowledgment, part gratitude, and part looking forward. Here is your chance to consciously reflect on the journey you took with your client and complete your professional relationship. Your client has successfully completed the *Academic Life Coaching Program*!

What

Another word for this exercise is perhaps *Reflection.* Successful completion has these five elements:

- **Mindfulness.** The key ingredient to a successful *Completion* is mindfulness – an awareness of the present moment. Mindfulness also plays a role in being self-aware of thoughts and emotions while reflecting on the past.

- **Assessment.** You ask your client to do a self-assessment using a *Wheel of Life* (Chapter 5) to identify how the *Academic Life Coaching Program* has had an impact on the different areas in her or his life. You also ask your client to assess the program and your performance as a coach.

- **Acknowledgment.** You lean into the skill of Acknowledgment (Chapter 7) to give your client a heartfelt acknowledgment about the character strengths you see in him or her.

- **Design the alliance.** You can do a quick *Design the Alliance* (Chapter 2) to design with your client how you want to build your relationship in the future. For example, you can make a plan to check in every three months or so to see how the Leadership Project or college application went.

- **Gratitude.** *Completions* usually end in shared gratitude, with the coach and the client thanking each other for a valuable experience.

Why

- **Serves as a mini-graduation ceremony.** *Completion* serves as a mini-graduation ceremony. It is time you set aside to reflect on accomplishments, as well as being mindful of the present moment. Setting aside such time helps the program feel complete and your client to feel a sense of accomplishment.

- **Assessments help accountability.** An assessment provides a benchmark to judge whether or not the action was effective. The *Wheel of Life* is an easy way to help your client make a quick assessment and see how far he or she has come since the beginning of the program.

- **Reflects on the professional relationship & designs the future.** A mindful *Completion* gives you and your client the opportunity to reflect on the professional coaching relationship, what was useful, what could be better, and what you and your client have learned from your time together. *Completion* is also powerful because you have the opportunity to discuss how you can best support your client moving forward and what you want your future relationship to be like. (It's great when former clients check in from time to time!)

How

1) Consciously take a moment to reflect back on the program. Ask your client to do the same.

2) Determine what you need to complete the program and the professional relationship. You play an important role in your client's life. Your words matter. Acknowledgment is a powerful tool for moments such as these.

3) Tap into gratitude. Thank your client.

4) Ask your client what he or she wants to say.

5) Offer your congratulations. Your client has successfully completed the *Academic Life Coaching Program!*

Conclusion

Thank you for completing this training! Academic Life Coaching offers a new perspective on education. Instead of cramming in facts and taking tests, this program focuses on personalized training. Instead of assigning specific work to students, this program gives you tools to help your clients create personalized assignments for themselves.

Success as an Academic Life Coach doesn't require complete mastery of each of these concepts as much as a mastery of trust (i.e. trusting your client to be naturally resilient). Your success requires you to be comfortable with failing and open to learning.

The purpose of the *Academic Life Coaching Program* is not for every student to reach a high level of competence in each concept. Rather it is about helping students find those two or three concepts that work well in their lives. Often when working with students and asking them their favorite concepts in the program, I am surprised which skills they select. Such a mindset shifts us away from thinking on an industrial scale, where every part is essential for function to thinking more on an artistic scale. The process is not as linear as it seems, but rather a cycle of growth, setback, learning, action steps, and then more growth. Once you start thinking on an artistic scale, new opportunities will arise. You can rework these concepts, combine them, and experience them in different settings under different circumstances.

Fortunately, we are living in an era when communication is easier than ever via email, blogs, and tweets. The world of education needs your voice and your unique experience. I invite you to share your experience and be involved in the community of those educators passionate about education and Academic Life Coaching. We are part of a movement to help young people receive a different kind of training that has an exponentially positive impact on the rest of their lives.

Made in the USA
Lexington, KY
18 September 2019